Outnumbered

Outnumbered

Memoir of a Schnauzer Mom

Isabel MacRae Allen

Published by Stonehill Productions, Inc.
Hendersonville, North Carolina
www.stonehillproductions.com

Cover design by Pamela Warr.
Cover photograph by Graham A. Morrison and Helen Moore.

ISBN-13: 978-0692462157
ISBN-10: 0692462155
Library of Congress Control Number: 2015943251

To Margaret Clayton,
an independent woman
and
animal lover

In loving memory of
Larkin Thacker Thompson

Contents

Chapter One
The Gooses

"It seems to bother people that I'm living alone in the Appalachian Mountains without a cat, a dog, or a man," I commented, while lunching with friends at On the Veranda.

Our waitress leaned in closer and said, "You're just smarter than the rest of us!"

Two years ago I'd moved from Atlanta to Highlands, a hamlet built on a mountain top in North Carolina. I was drawn to the area's natural beauty—blue mountains, waterfalls, fields of soon-to-be Christmas trees, rolling green valleys, and dark glades of ferns. Blissfully unaware of the challenges of mountain living, I'd longed for the peace and quiet of a small town.

Highlands is a summer resort an hour and a half west of Asheville. During the long winter months, it makes the ghost towns of the Old West seem populated. Eventually, I'd come to love the beauty of our winters. But now that I'd endured two, I needed company. My reasoning was overly simplistic: Cats came with litter boxes so they were excluded. Men my age came with more baggage than litter boxes so they were out.

What about a dog? In the past I'd owned a dachshund, a Spitz, and a Labrador retriever. These family dogs entered my life as puppies, but it had been more than twenty years since the last one arrived on a Christmas morning to be the dog of my daughter's childhood.

Nell and Bill Martin, friends at The Episcopal Church of the Incarnation, had a schnauzer named Betty Beau that they'd purchased from a local breeder. I agreed that Betty Beau was a marvelous dog. She was cute, incredibly clean, and weighed a reasonable twenty-five pounds. When Nell mentioned that her breeder would keep Betty Beau when she went out of town, my search was over. I loved the idea of my puppy visiting with its mom periodically and freeing me to travel as much as I wished.

So I called Nell's breeder, Sadie Persons. She told me that two litters of schnauzers were expected to arrive around the first of March.

"What are you lookin' for?"

"I think I'd like two puppies. Perhaps one could be silver, that stunning color of Betty Beau."

"Can't promise. It's in the Lord's hands," said Sadie.

I had a tendency to over-empathize with a dog left at home or in the kitchen overnight. Two puppies would keep each other company and relieve me of guilt. After I answered a few more qualifying questions to convince Sadie that I wasn't Cruella de Vil, she agreed to put me on the waiting list.

In the meantime, I had a little chat with myself. I had a deep desire to nurture that was digging a hole in my heart as I trudged along as an empty-nester. Also, I was aware that I gave too much in relationships and had to caution myself not to do that with the puppies. Whether it was dogs or people, my behavior was the same. I knew that I'd be the one in charge, the decision maker. But my emotions got me in trouble. Although I could see reason, I didn't always act upon it. If I could put myself first in this canine relationship, it would be a life-altering choice.

I saw dog ownership as a long-term commitment; a friend had had a schnauzer that lived to be twenty-two years old. If the puppies lived that long, they might become part of my estate. Furthermore, no one would have called me a dog-person, and I knew I'd never claim a dog as my best friend. However, having endured two divorces, I did see my new family—one that couldn't be broken—as the schnauzers and me. We'd grow old together.

#

A few weeks later, Sadie called to say both litters had arrived. The standard schnauzers on March first and the miniatures the following day. I could pick mine up on April 15th. It was the perfect time of year to adopt puppies. For the following six months, the weather would be mild and before the snow began to fall, the Gooses would be housebroken. As we chatted, I glanced out the window and saw the forsythia in bloom. A wall of yellow banked the backyard. At last, spring was dawning.

"You need to choose your puppies so the next person on the waitin' list can pick his. Now there's only one pup that'll have the adult colorin' you wanted—silver like Betty Beau. 'Course he's black now," Sadie said.

"Okay, I'll take him."

"He sleeps on his back," she added with dismay.

"He'll be great! I bet he's a character."

I pictured the litter of puppies all scrunched up to their mother nursing while off to the side was a puppy sleeping on his back, little legs curled in the air, dreaming of his future home.

"He's in the litter of standard schnauzers like Betty Beau. Do you want another from that litter?"

"Yes, I think so. How about the largest female?"

"She's a long one. Right now her coat is white and black. That's salt and pepper when she's grown."

"She'll be fine."

"Do you have e-mail?" Sadie asked.

"Yes," I said, a little surprised that she did.

"Give me your address and I'll send you their pictures."

I hurried upstairs to my office and turned on the computer. After a few clicks, I saw my puppies. Both were the size of the little child's hand that held them. They curved around their hands in a fetal position. Just two days old with their eyes still closed; the male was smaller and darker than the female. I e-mailed the photos to my family and friends who lived out of town. Then I printed them and put them in my purse to share with anyone who'd like to take a peek.

The name *Gus* came to me after I saw his photograph, and *Lucy* was a gift from Nell's husband, Bill. When he suggested it, Nell was standing nearby and said, "I love Lucy!" The television program by the same name had been my favorite when I was a child. I wanted to grow up to be that zany redhead who exuded personality and had so much fun.

#

The weeks of waiting seemed to pass more slowly for Nell than for me. She had been hinting that she wanted to visit the puppies. So I agreed. As we drove down the mountain, we saw a few crocuses and grape hyacinths in bloom. There were patches of grass along the roadside in the lower elevations. We drove along Route 64 East to Cashiers and turned left onto Highway 107 North. Bouncing along in my Honda-CRV, we enjoyed the views of the green valleys as we talked incessantly. Nervous excitement gripped us. After a mile or two, we turned onto a dirt road that wound around in the backwoods. Like many private roads in the mountains, this stretch was only one lane wide. At the top of an extremely high hill I brought the car to a halt. The hood pointed skyward, blocking my view of the road. I said a little prayer that there wasn't any oncoming traffic, hit the accelerator, and over we went.

"That's Sadie's house," Nell said, pointing to the only one in sight.

"What an isolated area!" I remarked.

Her house was perched high on the side of a mountain. The front yard had been cleared mountain-style with only a few trees left and a rhododendron here and there. As I drove up the steep driveway, the tires spun on loose gravel. Sadie stood on the back porch with half a dozen schnauzers swarming around her.

After Nell introduced us, Sadie invited us inside. Her son and daughter were in the living room. One child was holding Gus and the other Lucy. The room was sparsely finished. I imagined most of their income went to feed and clothe the family of five.

A little red-headed girl looked up and said, "These are yours."

I carefully took Gus from the child's hand and wondered how anything could be so adorable. His body was covered in soft black fur, and his tan eyebrows and mustache protruded slightly, giving him a rather comical appeal. I raised Gus to my face and stared into his black eyes. I breathed in his puppy breath. I turned him towards Nell's camera, and she captured us. I was smiling broadly, and Gus was looking inquisitively at his new mom. Then Nell and I sat on the L-shaped sofa, sinking into the soft cushions. Fat and happy, Gus fell asleep in my lap. I rubbed his back with my finger and he moved slightly.

A few minutes later, I traded Gus for Lucy. She looked like an adult schnauzer in miniature. Asserting herself, she squirmed out of my hands and sat with her rear on the sofa, her body plastered up against my side. She fell asleep leaning into me, a novel position for a dog.

As I watched Gus and Lucy move around the living room floor, they reminded me of geese. I knew that Lucy was Lucy Goose and Gus was Gus Goose. The last name of Goose incorporated their physical movements—their unsteady waddling, their side-to-side locomotion, and the way they bumped into each other yet kept on crawling. This was who they were before they learned to express themselves in other ways. Together, they were the Gooses.

After we'd spent over an hour playing with the puppies, Nell said, "It's time to leave. We have to meet Bill at the Red Dragon Restaurant in town."

But I wanted to stay. Being part of the puppies' world had been delightfully uplifting. These warm, little furry creatures had been fun to watch and a joy to play with. I felt like a child who didn't want to leave the swimming pool late on a summer afternoon. Now I understood why Nell had insisted we visit the puppies.

During the past week there had been several deaths in our church family, another announcement of life-threatening cancer, and the toils of living in the mountains that get in the way of wonder. But in the midst of death, there was life. Life was what Nell and I were holding in our laps. Life was crawling all over us. The puppies represented the other portal of our lives that we had nearly forgotten. The time of "birthin' babies" seemed so long ago! These little creatures were freshly experiencing the world and kindling a rebirth of our mothering instincts, a beautiful reminder of our youth. In our period of Lent, Nell and I weren't just holding puppies. We were holding life—a wonderment of God.

\#

When April 15th finally arrived, I felt like a nervous mother-to-be. On my way to pick up the Gooses, I swung by the Dry Sink to purchase a Pimpernel tray to put under their food bowls. I liked my house neat and clean.

As I was checking out, I shared my mission with the shopkeeper. "Watch out for great horned owls at dusk. They'll see your puppies as their takeaway dinner," she warned me.

"Surely not?"

"Honey, you just keep a close watch!"

I was a city woman and this type of animal behavior was inconceivable—a large bird dropping from the sky and flying off with Gus or Lucy. However, I'd soon learn that owls, and the increasingly more prevalent black bears, were just the beginning of a long list of wildlife that might threaten the puppies and me.

At the age of six weeks the Gooses were about the size of a large hamster. Worried about keeping them safe on the ride home along highly banked mountain roads, I put the pad from their new dog bed in the bottom of a deep wicker basket and asked Nell to go with me so she could capture any escapees.

Driving down the mountain, we noticed dogwoods heavily laden with white flowers, and crabapple trees bloomed multi-shades of pink. In panoramic views the trees appeared bare. But if one looked closer, there were putty-green leaves, small mauve leaves, and ochre leaves. The scenery was a mix of winter and spring, of bright colors and subtle neutrals.

When we arrived at Sadie's house, Gus and Lucy were in the kitchen. They had been separated from their mother and littermates. After asking Sadie every question I could think of, she said to feel free to call anytime. I placed my checkbook on the cold, gray counter and dug in my purse for a pen. Handing her a check that rivaled mine from social security, I knew she was a professional whose interest in the puppies would continue long after they'd left the nest.

Nell hopped in the passenger seat, and I placed the basket of puppies in her lap.

"They're precious!" she said.

"Aren't they?"

We couldn't take our eyes off the little ones. Gus and Lucy climbed on top of each other in constant motion, looking like a black and gray braid. I started the engine and backed down the steep driveway, trying not to run over Sadie's schnauzers that were barking at the car. As we climbed the curvy mountain roads to Highlands, I glanced at the Gooses. They had settled down in their basket home. Gus gave me a wide-eye stare, and Lucy was content being caressed by Nell. After a few minutes, the hum of the road lulled them into a lovely sleep of the innocent.

Chapter Two
Conversion: My Kitchen to Their Kennel

Before moving to Highlands, I'd considered living in Europe and running a bed & breakfast. England, Italy, and France were at the top of my list. I loved the tranquil beauty of England's Lake District. I liked to speak aloud the names of the villages—Windermere, Ambleside, Keswick. I pictured rolling hillsides, charming stone buildings, and gleaming wooden boats resting on the grassy shore. I saw the ghosts of Wordsworth and Beatrix Potter strolling hand in hand "beside the lake, beneath the trees."

Also, I loved the lakes of northern Italy. Perhaps Lago di Maggiori or Lago di Como would be exciting, interesting places to live. To gaze upon them was to see the snowcapped Alps in the distance and palm trees beside limpid lakes, which was the most beautiful landscape I'd seen in my travels.

And then, there was France. I knew Paris well; I could draw a map with my favorite haunts—Musée Rodin, Musée Cluny, Rive Gauche, Ile Saint-Louis, and the Quartier Latin. As well as knowing Paris, I'd traveled widely in France. But being from Buckhead, the northwest section of Atlanta, that is covered in

English ivy, manicured lawns, and a vast variety of vegetation, I wanted to live in the lush Dordogne in southwest France. I pictured its namesake river meandering through villages of sun-kissed stone, a landscape of overgrown greenery, and wild orchids growing by the roadside. But I decided that it would be a more practical move to stay in the States where a church would be the center of my life and provide a pool of new friends. Alas, living in Europe remains a dream.

#

My Highlands house was built into a hillside at the end of a cul-de-sac. What I like best about it is the path of the sunlight as it travels through the day. In the mornings the sun floods the kitchen and office; in the afternoon it warms the living room and three bedrooms. The day ends with a glorious orange sunset behind the mountains visible from the front deck.

Like many mountain communities, my neighborhood is a mixture of summer residents, local people, and those like myself who have escaped city life to enjoy small-town living. Before moving, I'd envisioned myself eating locally grown vegetables and raising guinea hens. I'd let my gray hair turn white and rejoice in my wrinkles. Now facing the other end of life, I considered dying without medical intervention. And there you have it, a hopelessly overgrown romantic living in the mountains with two schnauzer puppies.

#

My first night with the Gooses passed quietly. Being a lackluster cook, I'd restricted them to the kitchen. I barricaded their way to the living room with a wall of old file boxes filled with Madame Alexander dolls my daughter Margaret had found uninteresting. In the morning I climbed over the boxes. The Gooses squealed. I sat down on the floor with them. I let them nip and lick and climb on top of each other and me in an ecstatic state of mind. How nice to have the little ones welcome me to the morning. I loved having my lap filled with soft, warm puppies. They were the reason why the schnauzer breed has continued for hundreds of years. They were irresistible!

After our lap party, I took the Gooses outside and put them in the sandbox I'd inherited from the previous owner. I loomed over them with trowel in hand ready to flick any little deposits into the woods. But the cold weather and dew on the sand gave them a chill so I brought them inside where I wrapped them in a blanket and held them next to me until they stopped shaking.

Feeding time was next on the schedule. They waited quietly as I scooped up one cup of IAMS puppy food. Then I gave them fresh water that comes from the neighborhood well. Lucy jumped into the water bowl, then into the food bowl like a piece of chicken being battered before it's fried. Gus was pushed out of the way, but acted like a gentleman as he stood still watching his sister. From that day forward, the Gooses waited patiently for their kibble.

As the weeks passed, the nights continued uninterrupted, broken only by my emergence into the kitchen in the morning. One night during a thunderstorm with high winds banging the house unceasingly, I hurried to check on the Gooses. They were asleep in their bed; one of Lucy's front legs was hanging out. I was surprised because I'd never owned a dog that wasn't frightened by thunder and lightning. Even in the early days of our relationship, there were subtle hints—quiet during the night, waiting silently to be fed, nonplussed by thunderstorms—that my schnauzers didn't resemble the other dogs I'd owned.

#

At two months of age, the only trouble spot for the Gooses was a large spathiphyllum plant in the kitchen. I entered their space one morning to find them standing in the pot—digging, their paws covered with potting soil. The plant now resembled a thin-leafed fern.

"Gus, did you shred this plant?" I asked.

He looked at me with a long leaf hanging from the corner of his mouth and shook his head, perhaps trying to consume the evidence. Lucy hopped out of the pot and came to me for reassurance. I reached down and gave her a pat on the head. Time for their first bath.

#

In early May, Sadie called to see how we were doing. "How's the trainin' goin'?" she asked.

Training? What training? Pictures of circus dogs with frilly collars jumping through brightly colored hoops flashed through my mind. I was the only one whose life had been transformed. Gus and Lucy were just being puppies. They ate, slept, tinkled, and pooped. My kitchen had become their kennel. If they could claim a room after just two weeks, would they soon take over the entire house?

As I held the phone to my ear, I looked around. There were almost more bark chips, dirt, and twigs scattered on the floor than outside. These items weren't just tracked in by eight little paws, but were brought in by the puppies. Sometimes in a mouth and other times stuck to a furry body. The Gooses saw the entire outdoors as a supermarket of delectable edibles.

Furthermore, they produced more than their body weight in waste matter daily. To tackle this mess I'd bought a new mop, wet-pads for the old mop, rolls of paper towels—that ecologically offended me—Odoban, orange spray, lemon spray, and Get-Rid-of-the-Dog-Smell spray. In the final flourish, I'd added Doggie-Go-Here spray and Doggie-No-Go-Here spray, but the subtle difference in the wording confused them.

As my conversation with Sadie was winding down, I was still at a loss for words to respond to the question about training the puppies. The only training my pervious dogs had needed was to be house-broken. As I said good-bye to Sadie, the UPS deliveryman arrived at the back door. He viewed the carnage and then asked, "What happened here?"

"Puppies. I have two schnauzer puppies, Gus and Lucy."

He smiled as he spotted Lucy waddling over to say hello. He reached down and gave her a pat. He handed me a small package from Chico's, one of my favorite stores. He must have been the only person in Highlands who hadn't heard I was adopting two puppies. The remarks had ranged from, "Aren't you smart!" to the other extreme, "How do you expect to potty train two puppies at the same time?"

#

I hoped that our first visit with the vet would shed light on what kind of training the puppies needed. I knew that my previous dogs hated going to the vet's office. Some trembled as we waited in the reception area. I thought the Gooses' first visit would be cemented into their psyches like the first day of school is for a young child.

After the receptionist at Dr. Ransom's office obtained all the necessary information from me, I asked about their emergency procedures. I was given an after-hours phone number. If the vet wasn't available, I'd have to drive to Georgia or South Carolina to the nearest fully staffed veterinary clinic. The prospect of driving on unfamiliar mountain roads while feeling distraught about one of the puppies filled me with anxiety.

The Gooses and I were ushered into an examining room and in a few short minutes, the vet's assistant arrived. One of my pet peeves is a professional who doesn't introduce herself. An introduction not only gives me the courtesy of knowing the person's name, it also tells what she's getting ready to do. There had been no introduction.

The assistant reached in the crate and took Lucy out. Then she reached deep inside and tried to pull Gus out by the scruff of his neck. He yelped!

"Please don't do that! I'll get him out," I said. I crouched on all fours, looked Gus in the eye, and patted the floor. He gave me a worried look as he came out, as if to say, "What was that all about? I'm ready to leave."

After the assistant weighed the puppies and took their temperatures, Dr. Ransom arrived to exam them. He was short and balding with sparking blue eyes. Both dogs stood up tall on the stainless steel examining table while he checked them out. Surprising me, they'd assumed the stance of a Westminster show dog, their leashes hooked to a high steel bar.

Dr. Ransom asked a lot of questions in rapid secession. When he finished, he said, "I'm very impressed with their comportment. They are beautifully behaved dogs."

"Thank you. My breeder, Sadie, and her three children handled the puppies from the day they were born. They're used to human contact."

"That's wonderful. Sometimes the breeder puts his finger in the newborn's orifices—their mouth, ears, and their anuses."

Was he suggesting that I do the same?

"I think you've made a good choice. They'll have a lot of energy for the first year or so. But you're a calm person and that will rub off on them."

"Let's hope so," I responded.

"These dogs are a great match for someone your age. You'll enjoy them long into your dotage."

Because he was my age, I wasn't offended and changed the subject. "What house-breaking method do you recommend?"

"Crate training is very successful. Before you leave, I'll give you a handout that explains it in detail."

"Thank you."

"But you must remember, who's the alpha-dog?"

"Who?"

"You, of course!"

"*Me?*"

"Yes. You mentioned that it's been twenty years since you raised a pup. Well, you have a lot to catch up on, Alpha-dog."

When I'd adopted the Gooses, I hadn't planned on becoming any kind of dog. Furthermore, my life was full. I expected the puppies to fall in line like good little soldiers marching in step. In my younger years I'd been a wife, a mother, a single parent, a stepmother, a horsy mom, a grad student, a math teacher, a carpool driver, a cook, a bottle washer . . . and now in my golden years I was the home owners' association president, the Literacy Council tutor, the Food Pantry volunteer, the Counseling and Psychotherapy Center board member, an eternal student who took all the Center for Life Enrichment classes I could afford, an oil painter, a writer, and more. But I forget. And now, the alpha-dog.

Overall, we'd had a very nice visit with Dr. Ransom. I loaded the Gooses's crate into the car and put *Pachelbel's Greatest Hits* into the CD player. I "sang" along as I drove up the mountain, suppressing a desire growing out of my new role—to bay like a coonhound.

#

My backyard is a narrow, level strip of land with an eight-foot wall of dirt that rises gradually to the woods beyond.

As I sat in the sandbox with the puppies, I noticed that the delicate spring leaves had popped out on the hardwoods. The jonquils next to the back door were in bloom and the hostas had reappeared. Grass and ferns gave added color to the carpet of brown leaves that hugged the mountainside in May.

Owning the puppies had brought me outside, and as always, I found just being there quite peaceful. The Gooses' desire to explore the great outdoors—the allure of scents, the feel of weeds, the taste of grasses—was a strong, innate pull for them. They loved being in the yard. At the same time, there was a hazy thought forming in the back of my mind: They need to learn the scents of danger in the woods of Appalachia.

Mr. Peters, my next-door neighbor, had arrived to meet the puppies. He was about eighty years old, tall and thin with an unruly mop of white hair. He was wearing overalls and a freshly laundered white t-shirt that had a sweet scent. Because he had a pack of blue tick hounds, I wondered what he'd think of my gentrified schnauzers.

"What kind of dogs are 'em?" he asked as he sat down in the sandbox, his long legs folding up neatly.

"Them's . . . they're schnauzers," I said.

"Sounds German. 'Em Nazi dogs?"

"No, they've had all the Nazi bred out of them," I assured him.

"You got a male and female?"

I nodded. Lucy was climbing out as Gus looked on. His little black eyes weren't hard to read: I want to climb out, too. I reached for Lucy and caught her under her soft tummy then returned her to the sandbox. The Gooses began to sniff and dig. A few new leaves blew in and they waddled over to examine them. When Lucy bit into a dried oak leaf, it crackled in protest.

"Bet you named 'em Frankfurter and Brunhilda." Mr. Peters tossed his head back and laughed.

"The gray one is Lucy, and the black one is Gus."

"Why do you city folks give dogs people names? Whatever happened to Spot, Rover, and Fluffy? You kinda look like a woman who would name her dog Fluffy."

I smiled sweetly, suppressing the desire to point out that neither dog had spots, and Rover hinted of the fifties. But I did look like a woman who might have named her dog Fluffy.

"I bet you buy 'em clothes!" Mr. Peters dissolved into laughter, rocking back and forth on the tiny triangular seat. "I bet you dress 'em up for Halloween and put them in the town's Parade of Pets! I can see it now. Little Lucy can be a witch and Gus can go as a ghost."

"Dressing them for Halloween is a great idea!"

Mr. Peters stood up, brushing sand off his overalls with deeply wrinkled hands.

"You be sure to bring 'em by our house to Trick or Treat. Mrs. Peters won't believe this," he said, shaking his head. "City folk!"

Chapter Three
The New Boarders

As spring turned to summer, the flame azaleas and pink mountain laurel bloomed down the hillsides. The days were balmy and the nights chilly, typical of early June. I found that I was spending even more time outdoors with the puppies and loved being with them. I watched as they felt their first raindrops, ran around in puddles, and lapped the early morning dew. I watched when they heard their first barking dog. When I opened the back door to the blackness of night, the puppies jumped down the doorstep and stopped dead in their tracks. What had happened to their world? Where had it gone? I watched as they learned to run—pure joy! But when they tried to stop, they tumbled and fell. It was exhilarating to see simple things through their eyes, and to find that their fresh perspective on life enriched mine. The old and familiar became new and awe-inspiring.

It was fascinating to watch their different personalities emerge. Lucy's adjustment to her new surroundings was more difficult than Gus's and she seemed more focused on me. As the first few weeks passed, Lucy went from being subservient to

Gus to being the dominant dog. When it came to investigating the world, she was adventurous and fearless. She was the first to climb the back porch steps. When she tried something new, Gus might follow but overall he remained reticent; he had an intelligent vulnerability. He was *The Thinker*. When he couldn't reach the bottom step on the back porch stairs, he climbed on a log and stepped through the balustrades—a feat that declared his brilliance.

As Lucy pranced into the garage to investigate the eerie, dark room with unpleasant odors, Gus remained at the door. When I allowed them supervised play outside the kitchen, Gus refused to walk on my bathroom floor even though it was the same flooring as the kitchen's where he happily tottered around. As Lucy bolted up the carpeted stairs to my office atelier, Gus climbed the first few steps, sat on the landing, and awaited the return of his womenfolk.

As befitting a female, Lucy was the first to bark. She said *roo-roo* with an angry undertone whenever she didn't get her way, or whenever a new piece of furniture was brought into the house and placed on her floor. When she looked up at me and protested *roo-roo, roo-roo*, she'd shake her head. Her square jaw locked into position made her look just like Richard Nixon when he said, "I am not a crook!"

Lucy was a special soul. She was the first lap dog I'd owned. She had a way of collapsing in my lap. Sometimes she'd put her head on my thigh then look up into my eyes. I was hers.

"You're an easy dog to love," I'd say.

Lucy liked my tennis socks and picked them up as soon as I took them off at night, taking them to the dog bed. Gus, on the other hand, was a shoe and chew man.

When Lucy finished eating a chew stick at a speed that would make a beaver envious, she'd trot over to snatch Gus's. I'd hold her back and he'd give me a grateful glance. At other times he'd look at me as if to say, "Hey, she stole my chew again. Intervene!" I was delighted that Gus had learned to come to me for help; we were building a rapport.

Being the only male in the household, Gus found his individuality in aligning himself with President George W. Bush. His obsession with Bush began with his George W. doll, a bestseller at Whiskers on Main Street. Although the accompanying literature said the manufacturer wasn't expressing political views, George W. had a book entitled *English as a Second Language* in his back pocket. When I brought the President home, Gus and Lucy each grabbed a red boot and pulled, playing tug-of-war. When their play ended, Gus took George W. to their bed, where he stored his stash of toys, twigs, and unfinished chew sticks. I loved that Gus obsessively cleaned up after them.

Faster than the eye could see, the puppies would charge out the back door with one of their toys. And as you might imagine, this happened to George W., whom I assumed was lost in the ever-growing briar bushes. As Gus moped around in search of his male companion, my heart ached for him. He wasn't appeased until he had a new one. A few days later, Gus looked surprised when I swept the original George W. from underneath the sofa. Nasty, dirty but wonderful in Gus's eyes.

In the evenings when Gus had had enough of Lucy's bantering, I'd put him on the sofa with me. She was too short to jump up. Like the warriors of old, Gus had the advantage of high ground. Standing on her hind legs Lucy tried to nip him, but Gus went on the defensive, darting across the sofa. Inevitably, she grew weary and stretched out in the dog bed, happy to have it all to herself. And Gus, my boy, fell asleep on the sofa with me.

#

The town of Highlands was founded in 1875 when Samuel Kelsey and Clinton Hutchinson drew lines on a United States map from Chicago to Savannah and New York to New Orleans. They thought the two lines would become important trade routes and city of Highlands, where they intersected, a boomtown. Fortunately, neither happened.

During those early years, vacationers from hot, humid cities of Atlanta, New Orleans, Savannah, Charleston, and Chicago found Highlands a delightfully cool place to enjoy the out-of-doors, attend square dances, and just watch the fog roll down Main Street. People from the same cities return today, along with retirees from Florida and visitors from the Mississippi Delta. This year many of my family and friends would be among the hot, sweaty people coming to town.

Memorial Day marks the beginning of the season when walls of rhododendron with fuchsia blooms herald the return of the summer people. Our little town of a thousand balloons to fifteen thousand plus. I began to wonder how the Gooses would get along with my houseguests. What would my friends think of my un-house-trained pups? Would they trip over them and break a bone? Many of my friends were artists who came to take a weeklong course at our fabulous art museum, The Bascom. So I worried about handling my schedule, the guests' schedules, and the puppies' schedule. I was an organized person who didn't multi-task well.

Furthermore, approaching four months old, the Gooses had only two modes of behavior—wild and asleep. Whenever they escaped the kitchen, I could capture each puppy in one hand but they were quickly gaining weight. And they could run fast—faster than their mother. They were moving farther afield inside the house and outdoors. Complicating the situation, their ability to do certain things changed daily, but my thoughts remained cemented to yesterday's capabilities.

After exploring the rest of the house, the puppies knew there was life beyond the kitchen. They attempted to move and eat the file box barrier that restrained them. Failing with those strategies, they pushed the boxes around trying to get a gap big enough to squeeze through. Lucy was long and thin; Gus had wider hips. So she could get through holes that Gus couldn't. After trying to eat the armoire that stood between him and freedom, Gus squeezed under it arriving in the living room.

When the Gooses escaped, they were very quiet. In fact, the naughtier they were, the quieter they were. On one such reconnaissance mission, they retrieved Zulu and Rivity, a lion and frog in the Ty line of stuffed animals. Of all the objects in my second guestroom, which had been dubbed "the box room" on moving day, they had chosen the only animals. I thought this rather intriguing. The animals were just their size. They played with them for hours, moving them from room to room as they followed me around the house. As it turned out, the Gooses were the first dogs I'd owned that loved toys. Their favorite toy was the one the other was playing with.

Because the Gooses were eating their way through the file-box barrier, I decided to install a child's gate to keep them from entering the living room where they could destroy my sea grass chairs, shred the magazines tucked away in a wicker basket, and put their muddy paws on my treasured white chair once owned by my grandmother. As I screwed the hardware into the wall, I peered into the kitchen at Gus and Lucy who were sitting up tall—a full eight inches—in front of the television watching Cesar Milan on *The Dog Whisperer*. It was a stellar moment.

#

When I'd call the puppies to come inside, they'd stop whatever they were doing and charge side by side to the back door, sometimes circling under the porch before heading up the stairs for their treats. I wondered how they executed their synchronized moves. How were they communicating with each other? Moreover, I drew the logical conclusion: The Gooses would come when I called them.

One morning while I was entertaining my houseguest Kitty over coffee and scones, I realized that the back door was open. I hadn't seen the Gooses for some time. I called and called, but there wasn't any sign of movement in the tall

African-like grass of summer. Receiving no response in the backyard, I went to the front deck and called. I was standing in front of an opened sliding glass door; the screen to the door was closed. There was silence. Then I heard *whoop*. I looked down and there was Gus, sitting in front of me looking up into my eyes.

"Where did you come from?" I asked, turning around to investigate. "You've knocked the screen out of the door frame. You're a strong little guy."

Gus beamed.

My bookends were hardly ever parted so I was alarmed that Lucy hadn't returned with Gus. As reunion scenes from *Lassie Come Home* flashed through my mind, I ran down the long, steep driveway calling and whistling for Lucy. But she didn't come. As I came up the driveway, I heard Lucy *roo-roo*. I called and she *roo-rooed* again. I followed her bark to the garage and opened the side door. Instead of Lucy running out, I was greeted by a dark silence. Then I remembered that she didn't understand how doors opened. I looked between the door and the wall, and there stood Lucy with her little black nose pointing to the crack of daylight streaming in. I must have trapped her there when I had taken the garbage out. I picked her up and rubbed her gray, curly fur. She smelled a little like gasoline but was happy to be cuddled. When we came inside, Gus sniffed her. Then they hopped in their dog bed and slept for an hour, an unusual occurrence.

When it was time for a larger dog bed, I tossed it on the floor for them to play with. They flipped it over and caught Gus underneath. Lucy looked around stunned. Where had

Gus gone? Then she hopped on the bed! Gus emerged slowly, crawling on his belly. My puppies were clowns in fur coats!

Chapter Four
House-training

The standard schnauzer is the prototype for miniature and giant schnauzers. It is a German breed of great antiquity that became well-known in the States after World War I. Although miniature schnauzers are terriers, my standards are classified by the American Kennel Club as working dogs. Gus and Lucy were all muscle. Their ancestors were bred to be ratters and guard dogs. These traits surfaced when they chose the furry stuffed animals as their favorites, and their barking was so furious strangers were afraid to enter the house.

#

In July the puppies were eye-catching when they turned four months old. Gus arrested everyone with his dark good looks, especially women. But he preferred to play with men; perhaps he found them a novelty. Lucy remained a fluffy, curly, silver ball. Both retained their puppy shape.

I was so enjoying the Gooses, but I wasn't having much success house-breaking them. In fact, I was having more difficulty than I recalled with any of my previous dogs. If one wandered to the back door and sat quietly on the Heriz, I assumed he wanted to go potty. This happened quite often during the evenings when I was watching TV and had an unobstructed view of the door. Most of the time when I took one of the puppies out, he just wanted to investigate the out-of-doors.

I didn't care for the term, *go potty*, but apparently I had to name it.

"Let's go potty," I'd say enthusiastically to the one sitting on the rug and out the back door we'd scoot. I followed them around the backyard ready to scoop poop and give them a treat for a good potty.

Indoors, the puppies used the newspaper for the intended purpose about half the time. Some mornings when I arrived in the kitchen, it appeared that they had been preparing for a ticker-tape parade by shredding urine-soaked newspaper into confetti. Other mornings, the dog bed and toys had been moved around, giving the impression that a wild party had taken place. I expected to see them hung over. It was obvious that Gus enjoyed a party more than most intellectuals.

Nell, owner of Betty Beau, suggested that I stop using newspaper and try the new blue pads designed to house-train dogs. I agreed. I was looking forward to using them because the plastic backs would keep the urine from seeping through, and they would be impossible for the Gooses to destroy. Convinced that the pads would be foolproof, I drove twenty-five miles down the mountain to Walmart where I bought a box of blue pads. When I returned home, I cleaned up the old newspaper and sanitized the floor. Then I put a pad down.

In a stern voice I said, "Go potty."

"What?" their little faces asked. They stood side-by-side, looking up at me, their dark eyes blurred with confusion.

"Go pot-ty here!" I enunciated quite clearly, pointing to the pad.

"What are you talking about?" they seemed to demand. Lucy cocked her head to the side, emphasizing her lack of comprehension.

Well, my own bladder was about to burst after a couple of hours in the car. Perhaps I should have urinated on the blue marvel, because the Gooses never got it—even when I added Doggie-Go-Here spray. Every time I'd put a blue pad on the floor, they'd charge over and tear it up while I screamed, "No! Go potty! Go potty!"

After quite some time, I wondered if the Gooses had been hearing, "No go potty."

#

On a warm July evening, a couple of friends came over for drinks, a resurrected celebration in Highlands. The sun was setting over the mountains as we rocked in white wicker chairs on the deck while enjoying dirty martinis. Mine was a double. Old cast iron pots were planted with variegated ivy, purple petunias, and bright red geraniums.

I was entertaining Diane, who was an old friend and former dog trainer; and Carole, a new friend and owner of Lauren, a house-trained schnauzer. When the Gooses ran to the deck to greet them, Lucy went potty as soon as Diane patted her.

"Bad dog!" I said.

Then I gathered Odoban, another disinfectant spray, and paper towels. I returned for the clean up.

"Isabel, these pups should have been potty trained by three months," said Diane. "You must begin tomorrow before you've lost the window of opportunity!"

The phrase *window of opportunity* struck me with terror. Could it be that for the next twenty-two years, I'd have two un-housebroken dogs?

"My son Michael has trained his Golden. He can put a treat on his paw and the dog won't eat it until he says *release*," Diane continued.

"That's great," I responded meekly, "I've been trying to housebreak them."

"The correct term is *house-train*," Carole remarked kindly.

"You've had dogs before. How did you house-train them?" asked Diane.

"I taught the puppy to go potty on newspaper. Then moved the paper near an outside door. When he went to the paper, I'd bark and let him outside. Quickly, the puppy learned to bark to be let out. But my schnauzers are very quiet. Regardless of where I am in the house, they go to the door and sit silently."

"Well, crate training is all the rage," Diane said. "It is a no-fail method of house-training dogs. Dogs love their crate. They are den-like enclosures that provide the dog with a feeling of security. This feeling stems from his ancestors that sought caves for safety. When you get up in the morning, you take the puppies outside to potty. Feed them breakfast and take them out again. Put them in the crate for an hour; let them out on the hour. If they potty, they can play for a while. If not, back in the crate."

"It sounds like the Gooses will spend all day in a crate," I said.

"Not a problem! They'll love it there. Remember: Their crate is their cave!" Diane advised.

"Do you have a crate?" asked Carole.

I answered in the affirmative and brought it to her. It was an airline carrier, enclosed on all sides with a handle on the top. When I put it on the floor, Gus and Lucy scurried in, happy to be there. They turned to face us, their little raspberry tongues hanging out.

"This is a carrier crate. What you need is a pen," Diane said.

"I thought I needed a crate to crate train them."

"No, you need a pen to crate train them. A pen has wire sides and a pull-out bottom tray," Carole continued.

#

Dr. Ransom's handout on crate training said dogs wouldn't eliminate where they slept. The no-poop-where-you-sleep mandate was the golden rule of crate training. It was ingrained in every dog's psyche. The owner should never worry about his dog depositing urine or poop in the pen. Furthermore, the instructions stated how many hours the puppies could hold their bowels and urine at various ages regardless of their size or breed.

Was it healthy to hold it? Would all-of-this-holding-it have a detrimental effect on their long-term health?

Putting my trust in Diane's advice, I made a five-hour round-trip to Pet-Smart in Atlanta where I purchased a pen. During my road-trip, I had to admit that the old term *house-break* had taken on a whole new meaning. Lately, the Gooses had left little teeth marks in the cross bars of a Pembroke end table and chewed a corner off the Chinese coffee table. Surreptitiously, they were eating an arm on an old green sofa down to its wooden frame; bitter apple spray only increased the mastication.

Arriving back in Highlands, I was pleased to see the assembly instructions for the pen were easy to follow. First, I needed to attach the sides to the bottom grid. As I aligned them, the metal sides banged on the floor, and the frightened puppies hopped on their green sofa; they seemed to enjoy the higher vantage point. A few more bangs on the floor and the pen had become a loud, scary thing, and not a soothing, protective cave. Although the Gooses had gone into their crate of their own free will, they established the pen as *verboten*, true to their German roots.

The next morning I outfitted the pen with their favorite blanket and toys. Then I put them in it. I looked down at two little caged creatures. The natural sparkle in their eyes dulled by incarceration. I tried to be strong. I tried not to think of the pen as a cage but it sure looked like one. I'd never seen them so unhappy as if they were saying, "We liked it better when we had free run of our kitchen."

"I'm in charge. The alpha dog. The vet says crate training will work well for all of us."

I let the Gooses out to potty every hour. By noon everything was progressing nicely. So I decided to run a few errands. When I returned home, I opened the back door and for the first time since I'd adopted them, I was greeted by silence. Then I smelled poop.

The Gooses were mortified. They remained still, silent, and encased in poop.

I changed clothes and filled up the kitchen sink. Put on rubber gloves. I took one puppy out at a time and bathed each with baby shampoo. Then I took the bottom tray out of the pen, grabbed the dishwashing detergent, and went outside. I squirted the detergent on the tray, and then from a distance of six feet I hosed it off as my stomach did flip-flops. I tossed the blanket and toys into the washing machine. This clean up was far worse than wiping the poop off the floor and then sanitizing the spot.

Later that day, I was driving to a board meeting when I saw my neighbor Joy walking her two shih tzus. She had been interested in the Gooses' development. So I stopped and told her about the puppies' irreverence for the golden rule of crate training.

"Dogs don't read the books written about them!" Joy remarked.

#

I realized that I needed to know more about house-training so I went on-line where I found desperate people telling the truth. In the early 70s, I had adopted my first dog, a dachshund named Strudel. I had asked the vet how to housebreak her. In his words, "Dachshunds can't be house-trained. The dog will train herself when she's ready." And she did when she was three months old. So when I read *dachshund* and *schnauzer* in the same sentence, I was alarmed. The article informed the world that schnauzers were the most difficult breed to house-train. Furthermore, the inability to house-train dogs was the number one reason for giving them away. I could understand that, but couldn't imagine parting with my puppies. We were a family and we'd grow old together.

Shaken but focused, I continued to search for an alternative to crate training when I happened upon the Umbilical Cord Method. It was touted as fail-proof. It suggested that I tie a leash to my belt and secure the puppy on the other end. I was to go about my daily chores and when the puppy began to squat, take him outside. After a few days, the dog would be house-trained. I pictured this method working well with large dogs that took awhile to squat, but the Gooses were up one second and down the next. Their elimination system was about two inches from the floor. Instead of keeping them on the hardwoods as I'd been doing, now they were to walk throughout the house on the *carpet*. Carpet seems to call out to dogs: "Come hither, urinate on me. It'll soak in and you won't get your paws wet. Mother Goose will never know."

In addition to searching on the Internet, I read the following books on dog training: *Cesar's Way,* by Cesar Millan; *How to be Your Dog's Best Friend,* by the Monks of New Skete; and a little-known Walmart book on raising puppies that the breeder had recommended. I noticed none of the books explained how to train two puppies simultaneously. One owner to two dogs, outnumbered? As I searched the pages of a bestseller, I glanced up and saw a puddle that extended under the piano.

"Gus, is this your puddle?" I demanded, stumping my foot.

The little black fellow gave me a blasé look.

"Lucy?"

The princess looked haughty and incensed.

Something told me the Gooses were going to milk this no-fault situation for all it was worth. So I scolded them both and took them outside, wondering if the job of alpha dog mandated a 24/7 patrol.

Chapter Five

Leashing Loose Gooses

In August there's a hint of fall in the air; it's a cooler month than July. If one looks closely, the foliage is beginning to turn russet, bright yellow, neon rose, and soft peach. The briar bushes were turning the colors of autumn vineyards in France—yellow, red, and purple. Soon they will lose their leaves, only to spring back with vicious aggression next spring.

The puppies were at the back door although it was unusual for them to come without being called. Lucy was licking blood off Gus's nose. I placed him on the sofa and rolled him onto his back. Lucy stood on her rear legs to see him, front paws on the sofa cushions. As I dabbed Gus's mustache with a wet paper towel, I realized his fur was too thick to push aside to examine his wound. Soon the bleeding stopped. Most likely, he'd been pierced by a thorn on a briar bush. I wondered how the Gooses knew that blood signaled something was wrong and to come to me.

They had turned into beautiful creatures. At five months they had acquired their adult coloring. The fur on their noses formed large mustaches. Gus's was silver and Lucy's white with a few black strands on top. Their "eyebrows" were an inch high. A streak of silver outlined the edge of their floppy ears. Gus's coat remained black; Lucy's was now silver. (Lucy and I prefer the word *silver* to *gray* when describing our hair color.) The fur on their paws had turned snow white. Gus had a smoother, softer coat than Lucy's. His black fur gleamed in the light. I loved to kiss him silently on the top of his head and feel his fur on my lips. He remained the underdog, and a part of me identified with any righteous underdog.

The Gooses had begun to thicken around the middle as they grew into the shape of adult schnauzers. When I rubbed their tummies—something Lucy loved and Gus endured—I could see that Gus had become extremely broad through the hips. At a later time, I could see him moving those hips to create Gus, Junior.

Unknown to the puppies, their center of gravity had changed. Lucy tried to jump up on the sofa with her usual amount of effort, which left her hind legs dangling in air. She looked back at them, surprised that they hadn't come along with the rest of her. With the change in their body shapes, both were fulfilling their genetic prophecy.

#

One evening while I was sitting on their green sofa, I glanced over at Gus. He was sitting at the opposite end, his bottom firmly planted, and his left front leg on the sofa's arm. He was focused intensely on the television screen. He was able to recognize dogs on TV, even the outline of a dog. He seemed to think horses were dogs, too. When a dog ran toward us and then off the screen, Gus ran to the window looking for it.

I went into the kitchen to get a snack. Gus quickly appeared and began to circle the perimeter, shrieking! It was the most terrifying scream I'd ever heard from man or beast. It was high pitched, piercing, and continuous. I imagined driving frantically on unlighted, unmarked roads through the mountains into South Carolina to Greenville's Upstate Veterinary Specialists. I thought one of Gus' limbs must have been dangling from his body or when I picked him up, he would be covered in blood. All these thoughts flashed through my mind in a split second. I picked him up and cuddled his warm, soft body against my breasts.

"Gus, my boy, what's wrong?"

To my amazement he stopped screaming. I examined him from head to toe and couldn't find anything amiss. Later, I wondered if the remote control had fallen off the back of the sofa and hit him.

During our next visit with Dr. Ransom, I asked about Gus's cry and he blew it off. After all, the puppy was fine. When the assistant who had tried to pull Gus out of the crate came into the room, Gus began to shriek.

"*Eeeek, eeeek . . !*"

Now we had Dr. Ransom's attention. The cold surfaces resounded the sound. Lucy stared at Gus as Dr. Ransom manipulated him into a submissive posture. Gus on his side with the doctor's hand at his neck, holding him down.

"This is serious! Your dog has a behavior problem, " shouted Dr. Ransom. "I know a few professionals I'd like to recommend."

This infuriated me. The problem was the assistant, not Gus's recognition of her.

"Now wait a minute!" I said, "I just told you about Gus's shrieking. I think this is how he deals with stress. Yesterday he knocked over a large ginger-jar lamp. The sound of it hitting the floor frightened him and he began to shriek. When I picked him up and held him, he quieted down. He was fine."

At a time in my life when I was trying to simplify, raising the puppies was becoming very complicated. The Gooses didn't need to be house-trained but trained. Crate trained, not in a crate but a pen. Now Gus needed a dog psychologist or was it a dog behaviorist?

What I did learn about Gus's shrieking was that something had traumatized him. Out of the blue, he had been hurt. Several months later, the breeder would wonder if the groomer had hurt him. The groomer would wonder if the vet had hurt him. And so it went round and round. None of the professionals had an answer, and I wasn't ready to put him in therapy.

After a brutal divorce in 1997, I had been diagnosed suffering from post-traumatic stress disorder. My therapist had asked, "What are you doing with your hands? Why are you fidgeting?" I couldn't keep them still. Eighteen years later, I can't keep them still, which makes me appear ill at ease and uncertain of myself. After Zoloft and talk-therapy, my rewired mind remains rewired. Post-traumatic stress is difficult to understand for professionals and laypersons. So I felt great empathy for my traumatized dog, Gus. In fact, his exhibiting symptoms made me feel less alone.

#

Eric, an old high school friend, had arrived for a relaxing week in the mountains. While he unpacked and took a shower, I dressed in blue jeans, a rose Foxcroft shirt, and a straw hat to shelter my freckled face from the sun. He came in the kitchen looking refreshed and sporting a large bottle of Merlot. He cooked salmon steaks on the grill while I made a spinach salad. I had set the table with plates embossed with ferns and pine cones, green and brown plaid napkins, and salt and pepper shakers in the shape of a bear. The centerpiece was a vase of dahlias set on a bib of waxy galax leaves.

I was grateful that neither dog had made a spectacle of himself. Lucy hadn't greeted Eric by tinkling on the cuff of his khakis as she did with deliverymen, and Gus hadn't shrieked.

After dinner Eric said, "Let's take the puppies for a walk."

"They don't exactly walk on leashes," I confessed.

"What do they do?"

"I'll show you."

I got the leashes and attached them to the Gooses' brightly colored collars. Both puppies jumped on their green sofa. They began to jump from side to side like Lipizzaner stallions, rearing up on their hind legs as they pawed the air.

"Oh!" said Eric "How long does this performance last?"

"Until I take the leashes off," I said, laughing. "Let's leave the dogs here and go for a walk."

"That sounds great!"

I *was* making progress teaching the Gooses to walk on a leash. The first time I'd put the leashes on them, they had turned to stone in the parking lot of the vet's office. As I pulled on the leashes, clients walked in and out of the clinic glancing our way. I was beginning to look like a dog owner who was owned by her dogs.

#

It was the last week in August and fall was in the air. I was pleased that Eric had decided to stay longer. Although our relationship had been that of friends, I think we were wondering if that was exactly what we might want for our golden years. Quite simply, a nice and interesting companion.

An Atlanta couple was expected to arrive at any moment. I was exhausted. The Gooses needed to go potty. I took them to the back porch and quickly attached their leashes. Lucy leaped to the ground and then charged under the porch. Never to return. So horrible was this thing attached to her collar. As I called her, she came closer. She encircled a foundation post, catching her leash between it and the porch floor. As she attempted to get loose, her collar appeared to tighten, which increased her anxiety and made her pull even harder. I needed to unhook the leash.

So I dropped Gus's leash. *Clank!* was the sound of metal hitting the wooden porch floor. "*Eeeek . . .*" he screamed once, then on and on endlessly.

I stared into his little black eyes. He stared into my green ones. I yelled, "Enough!"

The look on his face was utter surprise. And he stopped! Even if Gus was frightened, he never shrieked again. But his high-strung, sensitive nature remained part of his personality.

#

The next morning it was raining, and the wind was howling. I threw on my raincoat and took the Gooses outside before my houseguests appeared in the kitchen asking for breakfast. The schnauzers, instead of staying in the backyard, marched straight down the garden path to the driveway and into the street. I ran through the house and called to them from the front deck. Without missing a stride, they continued to gallop like racehorses. Their taste of freedom, coupled with their privileged life-style, told them life was just a bowl of cherries.

"Gus! Lucy! Stop, stop!" Not even a nod of recognition came from either dog.

I grabbed the leashes and an umbrella, and ran out the back door as I mumbled to a sleepy Eric to make a pot of coffee. When the puppies saw me, they ran towards me. Taunting me by stopping just out of reach. It was more likely that Gus would come and Lucy would continue to run. So I focused my attention on capturing him. As I approached,

Gus flattened himself on the asphalt, his strong body pushing downward. As I leaned over to attach the leash, he extended his neck and lowered his head in a turtle-like fashion. Every part of Gus that could touch the road was now on the road. He was a fifteen-pound schnauzer pancake. As I pulled on his leash, Gus continued to press downward.

"Gus Goose, get up! Get up! I've had enough of your bizarre behavior!" I ordered. But Gus didn't move. I began to jump up and down. I pulled on the leash, but couldn't get him to stand. I glanced down the street and saw Mrs. Peters sauntering along with the pack of bluetick hounds, about three dozen of them. None was leashed and all walked ahead of her in an orderly wave. None ran off to chase a rabbit. None thought: "I think I'll just stop walking, collapse on the street, and flatten myself into a hound-dog-pancake."

As the rain stopped, Lucy ran over to rescue her brother. When I leashed her, she jerked her head and ran into the front yard. Lost in the three-foot high undergrowth of briars and weeds, she was impossible to see from the street.

Mrs. Peters and the pack passed by.

"Hi, Mrs. Peters. How are you?" I asked. Being a mountain woman of few words, she nodded. She smiled as she glanced down at Gus. Her dull red hair was tied back with a yellow scrunchie. Her plaid dress dropped from her shoulders and wiped the street as she shuffled along.

Having struck out with the pancake, I turned my attention to Lucy.

"Lucy! Come here!" There wasn't any movement in the foliage, no sound from Lucy. "Come here, girl! Treat? Chew? Sirloin steak?"

I imagined she had assumed the frozen stance the chain leash caused when attached to her collar. By now Gus was in a sitting position watching his sister who had outdone him with her quiet theatrics. I picked Gus up and took him inside.

"Eric, please put some scones in the oven! And the Greek yogurt and blueberries on the table."

"Be glad to. Having puppy problems?"

"I guess you could say that," I answered, closing the back door.

When I returned for Lucy, I noticed Joy, my neighbor, who'd told me dogs don't read books. She had her two normal dogs on leashes.

"Are you walking the puppies?" she asked.

"Uh, no. I'm just looking for Lucy," I said, too embarrassed to admit the truth. "She's somewhere in this sea of briars."

I wasn't an outdoorswoman. The outdoors made me sneeze and itch. I'd rather paint it than experience it firsthand. *En plein.* Impressionist painter and colorist, Isabel Allen. As I scraped myself up the hill covered with long, dense briars and blackberry vines, I was wondering "Where are the snakes? The copperheads that are so prevalent. The rattlesnakes that grow to be eight feet long." The undergrowth prevented me from seeing the ground. Each step took more courage than the previous one. When I spotted Lucy, she stared at me. I stared back.

"Come on, Luc! The snakes may bite you!" She just stared back again. I picked up the end of her leash and pulled. She remained firmly planted. I called again, hoping I wouldn't have to take another step.

"I've given you a good home and high-priced dog food! I've had it!" She didn't move. I walked over and picked her up. She noticed the audience that had been watching her rescue and barked ferociously at the other dogs as she wiggled her way out of my arms. She walked on her leash down the hill to the street where she made friends with Joy's shih tzus. I waved good-bye and we walked up the driveway to the garage.

Lucy stopped outside the opened door. I could almost hear her thoughts: "When I go in the garage, Mother Goose puts me in the car for a hair-rising ride to the vet's office—some strange form of torture! Better not enter." So she lounged like Cleopatra on a bed of ferns, looking up at me with her lusciously lashed chestnut eyes.

I reached down and picked up her highness. As we entered the house, I was thrilled to see that the houseguests were enjoying breakfast and being entertained by Eric's adventures gathered from years of being a photographer for *National Geographic*.

The next morning the sky was Carolina blue, the temperature about 70 degrees, and a soft breeze was blowing. With Lucy leashed, I opened the back door. We flew through the backyard then charged down the long, steep driveway as I yelled, "No, pull! No, pull!" I was hoping the Peters were still in bed. When we got to the opening in the woods where the power lines were, Lucy jumped and twisted her head through her collar. Liberated! She charged down the path cleared by Duke Power towards Route 64.

I ran after her into the woods, over gullies, and into brambles that tore my old blue jeans before finally landing her like a football soundly to the ground.

"Got you!"

I smelled the soil, rich and moist. Lucy turned to face me, giving me her look filled with unmistakable attitude. Before she caught her breath, I put her collar on and tightened it. She trotted happily out of the woods. As we walked up the driveway, Lucy took a step and then repeated her twist in mid-air that had removed her collar and set her free. Undaunted at still being leashed, she repeated her moves: step, jump, twist, land. Step, jump, twist, land. All the way up the driveway.

I waved shyly to Mr. Peters who was hanging over his fence watching us. This behavior of Lucy's was indeed strange. I couldn't defend it. My clothes were torn and dirty. I had little bleeding scratches on my arms. Over my heavy breathing, I heard, "That snoozer sure is a peculiar dog!

Noticing my cuts and scratches, Eric suggested he accompany me on any future dog walks. And so the leash saga continued the following morning. We were feeling brave. We took the leashes off the coat rack, being careful not to let them hit the floor. We clipped them onto the Gooses's collars. After they spun around several times, we left the back door running. I explained that this form of exercise was called a walk for a reason.

"Cesar Milan, where are you?" I yelled, and Eric laughed at my silly joke.

Clearly, some instruction had been lost in translation. That afternoon we took the leashes down from the coat rack, and the Gooses began to dance. They jumped around with their raspberry tongues hanging out. Friendly little devils that wanted to go for a walk—at the end of a leash!

Eric and I exchanged surprised glances and a well-earned laugh.

Chapter Six

A Peaceful Repose?

As my favorite month of September dawned, Eric left for New York to catch a plane to Borneo. The world was filled with marvels, and Borneo with pygmy elephants, Sumatran rhinos, and bantengs preening themselves. I realized that I missed him greatly. It had been so comforting to have him here. To have the two of us facing whatever the Appalachian Mountains threw at us. To face puppy training with a partner, evening out the odds. As our visit came to a close, we pledged to do a better job of keeping in touch, and he expressed the desire to return in a few months

Many of the summer families had gone home, and the leaf-peepers had yet to arrive. The traffic in town had thinned out, and dinner reservations are easier to acquire. This small, four-week window provides gloriously slow days. Time to climb into a pair of worn L.L. Bean pants, long sleeve t-shirts, and break out my cashmere hoodie. To smell the first fires of fall fill the air. To watch the lone sugar maple on Chestnut Street display fall colors a month before the others. And, this

September, I needed to decide whether to have the Gooses neutered or not.

At six months old they looked too small to have surgery. Each could still fit comfortably in my lap. When Lucy looked up at me with her chestnut eyes, I saw the trusting puppy that I adored, and little Gus—terror of the neighborhood—was still deciding whether to trust me or not. To consider letting the vet cut open Lucy's abdomen and take out her uterus almost appeared cruel. A shaman in my writers group held out a simple solution for Gus. He said, "Tie a string around Gus's balls and in a few days, they'll drop off."

Well, this Buckhead matron doesn't tie a string around anyone's balls!

I didn't plan to breed the puppies and knew there were plenty of rescued schnauzers needing homes. I'd read, too, that having the puppies neutered would make for healthier adult dogs; they wouldn't be susceptible to certain sex-related diseases such as cancer. As my thoughts continued to bounce around, I considered letting the woman vet in town operate on Lucy and Dr. Ransom neuter Gus. I thought that a woman would be more caring with female sex organs and vice versa.

I called Dr. Ransom and discussed my concerns. He reassured me and suggested having both puppies neutered on the same day.

I hesitated.

Because Gus hated the vet's assistant, Gus hated the vet's office. Because Gus hated the vet's office, Lucy hated the vet's office. So I was worried about going to Dr. Ransom for their surgery. Yet, Gus's tendency to nip had returned and a ball-less dog would be less aggressive. While I was in my quandary, Gus eliminated on my treasured white chair in the living room.

"No, Gus! No! No! No!" I screamed, running into the room. He looked right at me, hind leg lifted, aiming at the side of the chair. Urine spurting out in a long yellow stream with the force of a fire hose. As my screams got louder and louder, his stream of urine went on and on and on. I abandoned the empathy that John Grogan expressed in his bestseller, *Marley and Me*. I now stood firmly on his wife's side of the argument when she said, "Let's snip those suckers off!"

Lucy was a different story. She would have to be spayed. Whenever I heard the word *spayed*, I pictured a backhoe scooping out a uterus. Her surgery would be a more serious operation. Yet, if Lucy came into heat, that might push me over the edge from dog owner to local shelter contributor. Finally, I decided for the puppies' health and my peace of mind, Gus needed to be neutered and Lucy spayed.

On Monday morning I loaded the Gooses in the car and off we went for their politically correct surgery. When we arrived at Dr. Ransom's office, I tried to get them out of the pen. Instinctively, they knew where they were and refused to leave. Anticipating resistance, I'd left the leashes attached to their collars. The door creaked open and I petted them, trying to coax them out. I put my head in the pen and spoke softly to them. They liked that but wouldn't budge. So I pulled Gus out. I walked him to the fire hydrant in the side yard hoping that he'd potty but to no avail, and then up the stairs into the reception area.

"Are these your babies?" asked Susan, the receptionist from behind the counter, assuming that I had both puppies.

"Yes," I admitted. I did think of them as my babies. The office was very quiet so I was able to ask all the questions on my list. I felt a little better. Behind me—and unknown to me—Gus was having an endless bowel movement on the carpet.

"Okay, I'm ready to take them back," Susan said.

I smelled something, turned around and noticed a trail of poop, but not before I'd stepped in it. Clearly, Gus's nervous bowel movement told me what he thought about just being at the vet's office. Oh, if he only knew! I handed the leash to Susan while telling her how sorry I was about the poop.

"Don't let it worry you. Some dogs eliminate every time they come."

"God, I hope not! I'm going to get Lucy."

Then I hopped towards the door where a client and her dog were entering. She stepped back, a surprised look on her face. In these post 9-11 days she'd construed my behavior as abnormal. I hopped again and let the top of my right shoe balance me as I tried not to leave any more poop on the floor. I grabbed for the doorframe. The young woman gave me a strange look and stepped back again. "I stepped in it," I explained. I hopped again and grabbed the outside doorframe. I scraped the bottom of my shoe on the wet morning grass before crossing the parking lot to get Lucy.

She wasn't happy to have been left alone and was still unwilling to come out of the pen. I reached in and caught her. I lowered her to the ground. When we entered the office, she squatted and urinated—a veritable Lake Pontchartrain. I apologized again to Susan as I handed her Lucy's leash and ran out the door.

I'd planned a trip to Chattooga Nursery. People raved about their vast selection of indigenous plants and trees. The owners, Jodie and her husband, had been in the area for many years and had degrees in horticulture. Although it was a long drive from the vet's office, I knew it would take my mind off "my babies" having surgery. When I arrived, I became so immersed in the beautiful displays that I forgot about the Gooses. I bought a few evergreen bushes for the front yard and kept busy for the remainder of the day. The time alone felt quite lovely.

In the late afternoon I returned to the vet's to pick up the puppies. After I paid the bill, they were brought out on their leashes. They were dithering around as usual. I was surprised that they felt so well.

Dr. Ransom handed me a small envelope as he said, "Pain pills for Gus. He might be sore."

Gus! What about the one who had been spayed? Where was that woman vet? I accepted the packet of pain pills for Gus and asked for some more for Lucy. I gently loaded the Gooses back into the pen that now had their fluffy, forest green comforter lining the bottom.

When we got home, Lucy threw up twice. At eight that evening I gave them their first food and water since the surgery. They were groggy, yet comfortable. I imagined the anesthesia was still in their bodies helping mask the pain.

The next morning the Gooses were restless so I began to administer the pain pills. They slept. I spent all day with them. I told them how sorry I was to have made them hurt. I felt their pain. Instead of stitches there were over-sized metal staples running down Lucy's abdomen and between Gus's back legs. Every few steps, Gus would sit down and whip his head around, looking for his balls. I kept hearing his unvoiced cry, "Where'd they go, Mom?"

Two days later Gus was a sweeter dog that wanted to be held and patted much more than before his surgery. He hopped on the sofa, then rolled onto his back asking for a tummy rub. His bark seemed a little higher and his tendency to nip was gone. Lucy appeared to hurt less and didn't experience any changes in her personality.

Life with the Gooses went smoothly until Thursday morning when Gus came to get me. Usually, he had to do this several times for me to understand his message: There is something wrong with Lucy. I followed him upstairs to my office where Lucy was reclining on the down-filled cushions of the most comfortable sofa in the house. As I entered, she knocked her stuffed tiger onto the floor. She looked up at me and barked roo.

"All right, Princess, I'll pick it up. You must be hurting."

This behavior was like her door phobia. She would sit in the back of the pen with the door wide open, refusing to come out. Gus had to go in and bring her out with him, side by side. He did this with such gallantry that he endeared himself to me.

This morning Gus tried his usual trick—he jumped up on the sofa and then down. But Lucy stayed put. If I reached under her stomach and lifted her down, it would hurt her. After watching Gus jump off the sofa several more times, I knew Lucy was too frightened to cooperate. After all, Gus was saying, "This doesn't hurt me so it won't hurt you." I picked her up gently and put her on the floor. To my surprise, the Gooses charged down the stairs.

By Friday morning, the puppies were back to normal. I noticed there were two pain pills left. I considered swallowing them quickly with a full glass of water, but decided to keep them on hand for emergencies. September hadn't been as peaceful as usual so I opened the freezer and reached for a pint of Häagen-Dazs dulce de leche. What a lovely way to start the day!

Chapter Seven
Little Joys and Big Challenges

The Blue Ridge Mountains form the eastern front of the Appalachian range, dipping from Pennsylvania into Georgia and filling Western North Carolina. Their name is derived from the color of the mountains—blue, a deep smoky blue. The October foliage reminds me of the years I lived in Boston and traveled around New England and the Maritime Provinces of Canada. Many residents admit it was their love of New England that brought them here in their retirement years. Even the traffic jams caused by the leaf-peepers can't dull our spirits when we look skyward in October.

The landscape is magnificent! I enjoy the subtle colors of the trees as well as the bright ones. The soft peaches, the rose hues, and pale yellows contrast in value with the deep colors of the burning bush, Bradford pear trees dipped in rich jewel tones, purple leafed plums, and sunset maples glowing orange-red. The trees are made more striking by the rain as it darkens the branches and cleans the leaves.

On a warm October morning, the rain thundered down with unyielding vengeance. I'd opened all of the doors and windows to feel a part of it. As I worked in my office, I felt as if I were young again in the years before air conditioning was the norm. I felt a sense of freedom not being in a perfect 72-degree bubble year-round. I felt a part of the land.

The seven-month-old puppies were playing indoors even though they were bored with the house they had come to know so well. They had found their way to my office atelier. Lucy had been a frequent visitor but Gus rarely came. When he arrived that morning his little black eyes looked alert and his body shook.

"Good for you, Gus!"

It was fun to have them visit. I hadn't noticed when Lucy came up the carpeted stairs and sat in silence behind my desk chair, but both of them playing were impossible to ignore. Gus put his head under a skirted table. His rear legs were rigid, his back shaped like a sliding board, and his curly butt facing Lucy.

"*Roo-roo, roo-roo!*" Lucy barked in protest. She was frustrated and angry, as if to say, "This isn't the way our game of hide-and-seek is played, Gus!" (One puppy would peek out from under the dust ruffle on my bed, and the other would try to catch him before he disappeared again.)

They were wet from their jaunt on the deck, currently their favorite place to play. Not only had it proven to be an outdoor room filled with potted plants for the Gooses to investigate and eat—they loved the sweet potato vine—but it was also their watchtower for the neighborhood. On the deck they were masters of the universe. The bluetick hounds next door and the two large dogs across the street couldn't get near them. Anyone who walked by or cars that drove into their line of sight were barked at as if they were the enemy. As far as the puppies were concerned, the UPS truck came directly from hell.

I was trying to teach the puppies discrimination with regard to their guard duty. Fortunately, they were learning not to bark continuously at Sam, my other next-door neighbor. He had been the paperboy for Thomas Edison. He said that Edison was too busy inventing to pay him. Mrs. Edison held the purse strings.

I was determined Sam would enjoy a peaceful stroll in his vast front yard as much as he had before the puppies arrived. So far I'd been pleased with the outcome of their training, which amounted to my yelling *No!* and if they continued to bark, I brought them inside. Also, I was conscious of living under Highlands's unstated mandate: There will be peace and quiet.

#

The animals of the Nantahala National Forest, which engulfs the Highlands Plateau, were so foreign to me that it was difficult to imagine them living here. And *imagine* was the keyword. When I adopted the puppies, I hadn't seen an animal more threatening than a cottontail rabbit. But I worried about the appearance of a black bear when I took the Gooses for a walk. I felt totally defenseless and wondered if they thought I could protect them from the predators.

When I arrived in Highlands, my friends told me not to buy a bird feeder because black bears can smell the seeds from miles away. It's one of their favorite foods. Although black bears are known to be shy and prefer to avoid people, I'd picked up a few important tips concerning coexistence. If I saw a bear, I should attempt to look larger by holding my jacket open or raising my arms above my head. Bears don't like loud noises or the sound of the human voice. So I should speak to a bear and back away slowly with downcast eyes, indicating a non-confrontational stance. I should never turn and run, because the bear might consider me prey and give chase. If I saw bear cubs, their mother was close by and would attack if she deemed them to be in danger. I'd heard of two incidents when a mother bear attacked a human.

These rules were the best advice from the area's naturalists, but predicting the behavior of a bear in a particular situation isn't a sure thing. I chuckled to myself as I pictured a few bears seated on a log and a teacher standing at the blackboard with a pointing stick.

"Okay, girls and boys, today I'm going to teach you how to act if you encounter a human . . . Teddy, pay attention!"

Although I was frightened of encountering a bear, I did want to see one from a safe vantage point. Living here has given me a deep appreciation of nature and a heartfelt desire to preserve it. One of my friends had seen a red fox in the snow on her birthday. Another photographed a mother possum with eight babies on her back. Many people have seen bear cubs at play and getting their first lesson on the subject of climbing trees. And others have been within ten feet of a bear; they broke all the bear encounter rules when they turned and ran safely away. A friend placed her hands on a sliding glass door and the bear on her deck placed his on top of hers. So close. Eye to eye. Highlanders marvel in awe at the presence of wildlife, and treasure the pleasant memories and are traumatized by others.

I knew that many neighborhoods claim a bear or two. A bear whose picture graces the mantle beside family photographs. Now that I was a third-year Highlander, I wanted a neighborhood bear.

One evening Sam phoned. He said, "There's a bear in our garage. He's gotten into a 40-pound bag of birdseed. You better bring the puppies inside."

"You must take a picture!" I squealed. It was the time of year when bears gorge themselves for winter hibernation.

When Sam called, the puppies were inside but they were acting strangely—even for them. They were barking as they ran from the deck door to the back door, non-stop. Although they hadn't encountered a bear before, its strong odor alerted them to danger. I left the puppies inside and went out on the front deck. I leaned over the railing stretching as close to Sam's house as I could get, but I couldn't see the bear.

"Ohh . . ." I murmured a few minutes later, as a beautiful black bear lumbered down Sam's driveway. Front paws reaching out to the asphalt. He was young and healthy, about four years old. His fur had a high-glossy sheen. His tan nose pointed his escape route to the woods. I was thrilled to see him, my spirits lifted! A magnificent creature that usually hid in the forest was now on parade. My brief sighting brought the unseen, elusive bears of the Nantahala Forest to life.

Sam's parting words indicated the bear would return because the scattered birdseed in his front yard was impossible to clean up. I waited a short while and then walked across the back porch to the garage and drove off to a dinner party. Electrified by my bear sighting, I chatted about it all evening.

When I returned home, the sun had set. My bear fervor was replaced by cold, hard fear. I could only see what was in the path of the headlights. Mauled to death would be a horrible way to die. I blew the horn several times then clicked the garage door opener. I drove in, blew the horn again, and closed the door. I got out of the car. Approaching the back porch door, I walked through a strong odor—pungent, earthy, and wild. In a way that had not happened before, my senses said *bear*. I opened the door to the back porch, holding my house key in hand and ran. Fumbling with the key, I heard the tinkling sounds, and finally it slipped in the lock. I stepped inside the safety of the house.

Gus and Lucy welcomed me home in their usual celebratory manner of jumping around and squealing, as if they were trying to say, "Thank goodness, you decided to return again." But now, they needed to go potty. I attached their leashes, opened the door, and clapped a couple of aluminum pie pans together. These pie pans were my weapons of defense against a bear that might weight 600 pounds. The puppies hesitated on the back porch; their sense of smell must have been on overload. I tugged at their leashes. They trusted me enough to hop down the steps. The back door light lit only a small area. I stood between the woods and the puppies, thinking that the scent of a human would deter the bear. I talked constantly to the Gooses. I listened for sounds of the underbrush being crushed, for even a field mouse sounds like a large animal when walking on dead leaves. I saw Gus whizz the nearest tree.

"Good boy, Gus," I mumbled, pulling tightly on his leash.

Lucy began her potty dance. She walked a few steps forward, squatted, then up on all fours, and a few steps back. Forward, squat, up, back. Forward, squat, up, back.

"Please, Luc, not tonight! Go potty!" As if she understood, she tinkled.

When we came inside, I gave the puppies chew sticks for suppressing their fear and obeying me. Then I built our first fire of winter, piling native cherry wood on top of fir logs. As the fire grew, I put on my pajamas and returned to the living room with a Joanne Harris novel, *Blackberry Wine*. I tossed Gus's orange comforter near the fire and the puppies ran to it. It had been an exciting day for us—our first bear. I read until the logs turned to ashes, enjoying the sweet scent of cherry wood. I put my head on the arm of the Sheridan sofa, closed my eyes, and fell asleep sitting up, just like Lucy.

#

The quality of my schnauzers that impressed me the most was their overwhelming goodness. Their hearts were pure and they loved me with that uncomplicated purity. They hadn't been cast in the same mold as humans. They could be naughty but didn't intend to harm me or another living creature. Even the word *puppy* seems to equate with vulnerability and unspoiled youth. So soft is that word.

I saw the Gooses in a very different light from the predators—the black bears, bobcats, and mountain lions, and many others. I saw myself as their protector. Should they always be leashed? Never allowed to run free? Never allowed to run? The dilemma of keeping the puppies safe from predators and giving them a life worth living was the most heart-wrenching aspect of owning dogs in the Appalachian Mountains. For years, these questions gnawed at me.

I asked Mr. Peters over to get his opinion. He'd dealt with his hounds and the animals of prey for over half a century. We sat on the deck, bundled up in jackets and gloves, drinking coffee and enjoying the fire pit. The sky was streaked with pink and icy blue as the sun set over the mountains. Gus and Lucy sniffed the cuffs of his overalls. When he leaned over to pat them, Lucy dribbled a few drops of urine that I wiped up with my napkin.

"I need to walk Lucy. Won't take long. Be right back."

I thought I'd attached her leash but when I opened the door, she shot out! Shortly, I heard her barking. I could tell from experience that she was on the street at the end of the driveway. Her bark was ferocious. A bark I'd never heard her utter. My new neighbors across the street had built an attractive structure to hold their garbage. I named it the bear feeder. Bears can claw into a Mercedes' trunk so I knew they'd be able to claw into its plywood back.

I hurried through the house and onto the deck. I saw little Lucy barking at a big black bear from a distance of about fifteen feet. The bear stood on his hind legs next to the bear feeder, holding a bag of chips.

"Oh, my God! Mr. Peters, look! Lucy's found a bear! What should I do?"

"You're not thinkin' about goin' down there, is you?"

"Yeah," I said meekly.

"Then let this be a lesson to you: You can't protect 'em dogs from a bear or a wildcat. 'Em puppies need to recognize the scent of predators."

"I know if I run down the driveway, Lucy is more likely to attack the bear, trying to protect me."

"Probably so. One swat from the bear can kill her."

"Tell me quickly—what can I do?" I screamed.

"Call her from the back door. I bet she'll come in. Come on," he said as he got up to accompany me.

I threw the back door open and screamed for Lucy. She barked a few more times. I waited for a pause, then called again. Faster than the flight of time, Lucy flew through the door! A sense of relief coupled with Lucy's supersonic speed gripped us with laughter.

"I guess Lucy decided a smelly animal the size of a car was too much to tackle!" As we sat down on the deck, I asked, "Would I be a better dog owner if I always keep the puppies on a leash?"

"Don't you think 'em pups had rather live a life with a little adventure than spend it at the end of a leash?"

"I guess so. But I worry so much about this."

"You know, 'em dogs needs a chance to learn about the wild things in 'em's own way. They'll remember 'em's scents and stay away. Had a little dog that ran up to the attic the first time he smelled bear."

"That's good to hear. I guess the puppies' brains are wired to help them survive."

"You got that right! You city folks love to come to the mountains 'cauz you like walkin', hikin', campin' outdoors, and 'em animals love the outdoors, too. It's their world."

"Their world," I repeated.

#

During our next appointment with Dr. Ransom, I asked if he knew of any dogs that had been attacked by a bear.

"In the past ten years, I've treated three dogs that chased a bear and were swatted. None died from their wounds. But the dogs were small, courageous ones like your schnauzers."

"I find that unsettling. What would you say the odds are that one of my dogs will meet another bear?"

"Can't say. If builders keep clearing land, we'll have more contact with the wildlife. 'Cause they're destroying their homes with each tree they fell. Our pets will be at a greater risk, too."

Taking into account the advice of Mr. Peters and my vet, in the autumn evenings while I planted jonquil bulbs in the garden, I let the Gooses play at the edge of the woods. Unleashed, they could sniff and search. They could use their instincts in a normal dog-like fashion and learn the scents of predators.

I allowed each puppy a mid-morning run alone, but for the remainder of the day they were leashed. Wildlife feeds at dawn and dusk so I never let them out at those times. If the weather was overcast or foggy, I'd leash the Gooses. If they hesitated on the back porch or hurried down the steps and froze with their nose to the ground, I leashed them. I learned to respect their reactions to the wildlife that inhabits the Highlands Plateau.

Chapter Eight
Grooming the Gooses

In November the Gooses were eight months old. Their personalities had been formed, and we'd gotten to know each other. They had met their vet, been neutered for better long-term health, and learned to walk on a leash. However, if I defined house-trained as never, ever going potty in the house—well, we were still working on that benchmark.

The Gooses were striking-looking dogs, in part, because of the highly contrasting colors of their coats. I continued to be impressed by how clean my schnauzers were. Most of the time, they had a pleasant, woodsy scent, and sometimes a chocolaty scent of freshly baked brownies. Their fur was beginning to block their eyes and mat under their legs. Curly fur encompassed their little round bodies making them look more like bear cubs than dogs.

The books I'd read on raising puppies said they were overdue for their first grooming. I'd bought a dog grooming kit at Walmart. The main component was an electric razor, which came with several comb attachments to vary the length of the fur. Also, I'd ordered *How to Cut a Schnauzer Perfectly,* a book that surprised me by being over a hundred pages and requiring the purchase of twenty-two tools. In the abstract, grooming the Gooses had seemed doable, but now my courage was waning. Even with another person holding them still, they were strong enough to wiggle. The most terrifying part would be aiming an electric razor at that centimeter-wide row of fur between their eyes.

As newborns, their tails had been cropped but their ears left natural. So they had floppy ears and not the stand-up pointed ones that balance a long schnauzer goatee. I had noticed the fur under their jaws dipped in their food and water. The water acted like an adhesive for food particles that eventually dropped off around the house. So I'd devised a cut that would eliminated that problem. I wanted their goatees cut short, their mustaches trimmed, and their remaining fur shaped up. The overall look I was going for was similar to a puppy cut for a French poodle.

I searched the area for a reputable groomer. The first one I called gave cuts that were as good as any Westminster champion with sharply carved eyelashes and double brows. She was booked for the following two months and refused to alter the standard schnauzer cut to fit my specifications. The second groomer I spoke to said that she was booked for the foreseeable future, but she had a friend, Gloria, who had just moved to the area and was taking new clients.

I called Gloria. She loved living in this beautiful piece of heaven on earth and loved her clients from Highlands.

"Have you ever owned a dog that needed to be groomed?"

"No, I haven't. I owned a short haired dachshund that needed her nails clipped professionally, but the lab and Spitz were healthy and clean with just an occasional bath."

Gloria had asked the right question. I saw this as a good starting point; she was going to take me from ignorance to knowledge. She explained that schnauzers needed to be groomed because their fur matted, and they needed a sanitary cut around their private parts. She liked to groom them every six weeks.

"Would you give my puppies a variation on the standard schnauzer cut?"

"They're your dogs. I'll cut them anyway you want," she said, "Did you say they were from the same litter?"

"Yes, why do you ask?"

"Ah . . . how's the training going?"

"Not well. They usually come when I call them, potty outside, and Gus responds to the stay command."

"The dog show professionals have a rule: Never get littermates. They bond to each other and not the owner."

"That explains a lot. I've never had the feeling the puppies were trying to please me as all the dog books expound. They behave as an isolated unit from planet Schnauzer," I said.

"That's exactly what I mean," Gloria said.

"Can I make an appointment?" I asked, changing the subject.

"Sure."

The Country Squire, Gloria's grooming parlor, was in Franklin, North Carolina. A trip there mandated driving on either the dreaded Gorge Road or Buck Creek Road. Either

way, the journey would take about an hour. The Gorge Road
has extremely tight turns so one has to drive five miles an
hour to maneuver them. No one can drive fast on the Gorge
Road or he'll end at the bottom of the gorge. Yet, unlike many
people, I loved that road because of the spectacular scenery.
In November the vast panoramas of evergreens as tall as
skyscrapers are fronted by the colors of the hardwoods. In
the gorge the Cullasaja River rages over smooth gray rocks
forming waterfalls as it travels northward.

On the other hand, the Buck Creek Road has beautiful
pastoral scenery—red barns beside neatly plowed fields, split-
rail fences, wild turkeys, handmade signs announcing *Christo*
and the need to *Repent Now*. But it mandates a drive of over ten
miles on one highly banked curve after another. I decided to
take the Gorge Road because I'd be able to drive slowly and the
Gooses would have a smoother ride.

When the day of the puppies' first grooming arrived, I
loaded their pen in the way-back of my Honda-CRV and then
put them in it. On the way I sang to calm them, and when
my voice gave out, I played Gregorian chants. They were silent.
I concentrated on the glorious fall colors. I loved to see the
sunlight striking the leaves. As an artist, I love colors and
seeing the effect light has on them.

I saw the sign for The Country Squire and followed it
off-road. I parked and went to the rear of the car to let the
Gooses out. When I lifted the tailgate, I saw that they were wet,
covered in vomit. They were a pitiful sight. I had packed their
"diaper bag", an L. L. Bean canvas bag that held a roll of paper
towels and a spray bottle of orange cleaner. I wiped them off

then cleaned up the pen. I clipped on Gus's leash. He walked like a drunken sailor, did his express potty, and then we went inside. I tied his leash onto a mock hitching post then did the same with Lucy.

"You must be Isabel. Which one is Gus?" Gloria asked.

"He's the silky black one. Lucy is the gray one."

Gloria reached down and gave them a pat. Then she plucked out the fur between Lucy's eyes, showing me how easy it was to do. She ushered the puppies into the back room, the doggie spa. I heard the sound of babbling water and smelled the sweet scent of doggie shampoos.

"Uh, they're not completely house-trained," I hollered as I walked towards the door.

Gloria shouted to her daughter, who was up to her elbows in soapy water, "Hey, can you imagine that? Two schnauzers that aren't house-trained! Schnauzer owners should just tell us if their dogs *are* house-trained."

I liked that form of empathy. At long last, all the blame wasn't placed on me. Yes, I realized that Gloria's statement wasn't good news. I was still a bit unsettled after reading schnauzers were the most difficult bred to house-train.

When I returned to pick up the Gooses, they held their heads up high and pranced out to claim their mother. Each had a red bandana around his neck. Gus bit Lucy's; then Lucy pulled Gus's. They were about the same size; their gray undercoats were now visible. Lucy was soft to touch like Gus had been. For the first time, it was difficult to tell them apart.

I wrote Gloria a check—money well spent. She gave me stickers to put on my calendar so I wouldn't forget the following appointments.

"Thanks, Gloria. See you in six weeks."

The thought of my puppies throwing up on their way home seemed to negate the entire day. I knew that if they were in the front seat, they would have a smoother ride. I was determined to wedge the huge crate into the passenger's seat of my small SUV. After a couple of strong shoves, the crate was in. The standard gearshift protruded between two metal bars. I knew this was dangerous—especially on the Gorge Road—but I was willing to chance it. Some ancient part of my brain had taken over the normally rational one. I loaded the puppies in it, and then squeezed myself into the driver's seat with my right arm resting on top of the pen.

Being in the front seat allowed the Gooses to look out the windshield for the first time, and they began barking at the oncoming traffic. As we picked up a little speed south of Franklin before entering the Gorge Road, they fell asleep. When we arrived home, I was delighted that both dogs were clean and perky after their nap.

After hearing horror stories about bad groomers, and after having talked with a persnickety groomer, Gloria was a breath of fresh air. Heavens, I'd let her cut my hair and I wouldn't go potty in her salon.

#

The dark blue sky was filled with puffy white clouds, and the Gooses were loose. I was lopping branches off an evergreen when they charged through the yard, halting at the back door. I walked over to let them inside, but reeled at their scent and appearance. They were black and slimy. They smelled like a stagnant creek.

"Where did you find water? Couldn't you just have taken a sip?" I asked.

I was so undone that I sat down on the ground and cried. I couldn't figure out how to solve the problem. When my tears subsided, I'd decided to hose the puppies down. I aimed the nozzle at Gus and sent him flying across the driveway. He was terrified! So I attached his leash and wrapped it around the back porch railing. After removing the nozzle, I gently hosed him down. He stood still. Afterwards I rinsed off Lucy.

For months, I had been looking forward to an art show opening of Rosemary Stiefel's work. It was scheduled to begin in a couple of hours. Surely, grooming the pups couldn't take that long. I brought them inside. I put Lucy in the crate, and Gus on the sofa pad. If possible, he now smelled worse—he smelled like something dead. I rolled him onto his back and put a chew stick in his mouth. There was a grin on his face. I tried to brush through his fur, but couldn't. The briars were enmeshed in every inch of his legs and underbelly. I got the scissors and began cutting away little tufts of fur. When Gus's chew stick fell out, I'd put it back in his mouth. He was content.

After about twenty minutes, I swapped Gus for Lucy. I held her around her tummy, her legs kicking. Her curly fur was more difficult to comb. So I began cutting it. An hour later,

I could finally brush through it to remove the remaining small twigs.

I used rounded children's scissors to cut the fur near their eyes. Then I put them in the bathtub filled with baby shampoo, rinsed them under the faucet, and dried them. Their coats were only half an inch long and stood straight out from their bodies. They looked like they'd been electrocuted.

However, they were once again acceptable roommates. I'd learned that I could groom them in an emergency. But I'd missed the opening of Rosemary's show. The next time I saw her, I explained my absence.

"I needed to groom the Gooses or discard them entirely."

"I understand. Just before it was time for Bill and me to leave, our lab rolled in bear scat!" Rosemary said. "Bill had to bathe him."

"Oh," I said, picturing a dog that size coated in poop. "I guess I should count my blessings!"

One of the reasons I'd moved to Highlands was to have different life experiences, and many of these turned out to be rather shocking. And I'd just like to add, if you see bear scat, you know immediately the size of the animal that left it. One can't imagine what some dogs do with it.

#

It was a Friday night in late November, and the weather had turned cold. I was sweeping dead leaves from the back porch before going for a solitary walk. Mr. Peters and his brother Wayne were celebrating the end of a workweek. The guys were sitting beside a newly dug fire pit, drinking beer and boiling peanuts. In the background I could hear the faintest sounds of a Waylon Jennings song playing in the house as Mrs. Peters sang along in mezzo. I was surprised to hear the men talking about me and ducked around the corner of the garage to listen unobserved.

"Miz A. takes 'em outside and starts saying, 'This ain't no foraging expedition! Nor is it Morrison's Cafeteria. You need not eat grass and then throw it up back inside. I swear, it looks like spinach linguini.' She starts to sound a little pissed, but she goes on so sweet-like in her soft Southern voice. 'Lucy, why do you eat them rocks when you've got a bowl of high-priced dog food inside?'" said Mr. Peters.

"Somebody oughta tell her 'em dogs ain't never goin' answer," said Wayne.

"That's for sure," said Mr. Peters. "Yesterday I wanted to see 'em pups again. I lied down on the hill and waited. Knew it wouldn't be too long 'cause Miz A. takes them potty every thirty minutes—they must lie to her. Out comes Lucy, pulling her down the back porch steps. Lucy's got her nose on the ground and her's clutching the dirt with her front paws. Then hers head jerks from side to side like a Hoover vacuum cleaner. Our huntin' dogs have nothing over that Lucy when she trackin'! Right before Miz A. took Lucy inside, that dog grabbed a branch and walked through the door with it—just as proud as can be. You think she don't feed 'em 'nuff?"

"I tell you, 'em pups just keep getting' stranger and stranger," said Wayne.

Both men spoke in garbled agreement, hooting and carrying on.

"And for some reason she calls 'em Gooses. Gooses! No wonder 'ems confused!" said Mr. Peters.

"Sure 'nuff. I might better understand all this strange activity if she wanted 'em to hunt bears, but she jest wants 'em to shit outside!" said Mrs. Peters, who'd joined the party.

"You know, our cousin Gloria is Miz A's groomer. She can tell tales about 'em city folk who want 'ems dogs to smell sweet," said Mr. Peters.

"Dogs that *smell sweet*?" asked Wayne, his mouth hanging open.

"Yep," said the Peters in unison.

"City folks pay good money for that?" demanded Wayne.

I put the broom back in the garage, buttoned up my old barn jacket, and walked down the driveway. I was ready to meet a cool breeze, marvel at a few yellow oak leaves against an electric blue sky, and listen to acorns falling down like rain.

Chapter Nine

A Mountain Christmas

November had passed so quickly as if it had slid under the umbrella of "the holidays." I couldn't remember how old the Gooses were so I counted on my fingers—nine months. They were almost their adult size although they might gain another pound or two. Gus weighed twenty pounds and Lucy was close to twenty-five.

December brought problems that simply overwhelmed me. Visions emerged of the worst Christmas of my life in my exquisite Georgian house on Peachtree Battle Avenue where now my former husband and his live-in-lover resided. The usual drone blitz of family-family-family banged on the media while mine was gone. My bank account was overdrawn and the credit card attached to it was dead so the gas company refused to bring propane. And, if you can picture this, the furry creatures were eating everything although I was rarely a witness to their destruction. A living room chair covered in a charming elephant print had had the fringe ripped off its skirt. A treasured book about my MacRae family's history in North Carolina no longer had a cover or back. It never occurred to me to think: Today the Gooses might pull my eyeglasses off my bedside table. Up until that day, they hadn't removed anything from a table. I was shocked when I observed the schnauzers lounging in the living room gnawing pieces of quarter round as if they were chew sticks. Around the kitchen window the sheetrock had called out to them, "Eat me!"

On the surface, I appeared calm but clearly, I was having great difficulty juggling my life in the mountains with raising the puppies. In addition, I had so looked forward to Eric returning to the States; but the Arabs and Israelis were at it again and he was off to cover the Gaza War. I had a terrible feeling that my life was out of control; this had only happened once before. What I didn't know was that feeling would permeate most of the coming year. Foolish workaholic that I was, I kept thinking, "I can train the puppies by trying harder and stop the house destruction by keeping a closer watch on them." The worse things got, the greater my ability to regroup and try again. Without realizing that my attitude blocked the fact that I *was* doing well with my life. I had more than any one person could handle.

#

Christmas was four weeks away when I sat down at the computer to write an article for *The Mountain Laurel* magazine, an upscale publication. The mountain weather was outstanding. I loved the cold, crisp air of a December day. The sun shone brightly against the cloud-filled sky, making it look like a serene Corot landscape.

My daughter Margaret, who was thirty, was coming from Chicago and our cousin Larkin was driving up from Atlanta. I was hosting Christmas dinner for a small party of friends.

I hadn't decorated my mountain house with rustic décor of animal heads hanging from the walls, antler chandeliers, and twig furniture as many newcomers to the area had. I enjoyed the look, but my budget couldn't expand to the point of having all new furnishings as well as Christmas decorations that complemented them. Because I'm allergic to Christmas trees, I had bought a hand-tooled metal tree with alternating rows of reindeer and evergreens. Behind each one was a white votive candle that dripped onto the presents and looked like snow. I placed the tree on a chest in the living room so it would be reflected in the mirror behind it. The remainder of my Christmas decorating was placing stuffed toy moose and reindeer around the living room and stockings at the chimney.

The day after I'd decorated the house, I was sitting on my bed reading when I noticed Gus backing around the partially opened door. He had a red nose in his mouth that was attached to a reindeer just his size. Then came Lucy holding its tail! They had stolen Rudolph. When life looked dim, I could count on the Gooses to put a smile on my face. In fact, they put a smile on everyone's face—such a special gift in these hard times.

Margaret arrived the next afternoon with her Newfoundland puppy, Winnie. She was eight months old and the size of a VW Beetle. As they walked in the door, the Gooses jumped on their sofa and barked for all they were worth. Margaret and I laughed.

"She *is* a very large puppy. Newfoundlands are known as *gentle giants*. If the Gooses give her a chance, they'll like her," Margaret said.

From the sofa Lucy leaped onto Winnie's back, going for her neck. What courage! What optimism! The three puppies sniffed each other and jumped around some more. Margaret and I decided to let them get acquainted. We sat down in the living room to catch up on news about her new business. She taught horseback riding in a small town north of Chicago.

A few minutes later, we noticed that Lucy had become the alpha dog and all was well. Winnie curled up in the corner next to the warm stove where Margaret's chocolate chip cookies had finished baking.

"Would you like to take the puppies for a walk?" I asked.

"Great idea," replied Margaret.

We bundled up and took the three puppies outside. After a few minutes the weather changed drastically—sleet poured down and the wind was howling. We turned around and headed for home. When we started up the driveway, we inadvertently blocked the UPS deliveryman from leaving. Gus posed in the middle of the driveway—lying on his back with his legs up in the air. Lucy squatted near the man's shoes and tinkled when he patted her, fortunately missing his trousers. Winnie stared at the Gooses, looking quite amused.

As I signed for the packages, Lucy gave an unexpected pull on her leash and charged into the woods, skirting under the briars on the side of the house near Route 64.

"Lucy? Lucy!" I called but she didn't come.

"Do you want me to go get her, Mom?"

"No, I've had lots of practice at this." Because Lucy had her leash attached, I knew I had to find her before dark. It was five in the afternoon; there were only thirty minutes of daylight left. I asked Margaret to take Winnie inside and keep an eye on the back door in case Lucy returned.

During the past nine months, Gus and Lucy had rubbed each other's sides as they ran around in a way that made each appear to be a counterbalance for the other. This physical closeness made them seem more connected than twins. They reacted to the same stimulus in exactly the same way. I'd wondered if—in an emergency—one might perform the duties of a St. Bernard and find the other. I looked down at Gus. He seemed filled with nervous energy.

"Lucy. Lucy. Go find Lucy!" I said.

Gus ran up the hill in the back yard with me scrambling on my hands and knees with his leash held tightly in my fist. This wasn't the direction Lucy had run, but I trusted Gus. I began calling for her. I doubted she could hear me in this incredibly loud wind, but I didn't want Gus to forget the object of our search. I pictured Lucy with her leash entangled around a fallen log. She would be sitting there like a piece of bait. Bait in the darkness of night. Dead in the morning. Torn to shreds by a predator.

Gus continued his uphill run as I stumbled along behind him, stomping down limbs of the briar bushes, while calling "Lucy? Lucy?" Every now and then, I'd stumble over a large rock that punctuated the mountain landscape. Lucy's gray coloring rendered her all but invisible in the winter woods—a sea of grey-green trees, some needleless hemlocks, and ratty old pines. As we ran up the hillside, the tree trunks looked like a herd of elephants' legs.

Suddenly, Gus jerked the leash and ran to the left, up the hillside. With a few more turns like this, it was going to be difficult to find our way home. Gus jerked the leash and we ran left again, across the breadth of the hill. With each turn, we were going farther away from the direction Lucy had run. The sun had sunk but there was a brief afterglow. Sleet dripped from my face and I could see only a few feet ahead.

Gus saw Lucy before I did. His leash went limp. When I spotted her, she was sitting near a fallen tree limb with her leash entangled around its branches! Sitting silently. Like a piece of bait at the end of a fishing line. Waiting to be rescued.

"Good boy, Gus! Good boy!"

I stooped down and gave Lucy a quick body rub, dislodging the ice from her coat. Gus licked her relieved little face as I untangled her leash.

"Gus, you're really quite a dog!" I said, as I rubbed his little body, too. I felt so close to Gus. In some mystical, magical way, we understood each other.

The fallen dead leaves were now covered with ice that looked like broken glass. I was hobbling down the mountain with both dogs pulling me. I tried to avoid the briars while keeping my balance as I told myself the worst was over—Gus had found Lucy.

When we reached the embankment, I knew that I couldn't tackle it with both puppies leashed. I unclipped Gus and took a chance on him not running away. Happily, he ran down the hill to the back door and waited for us. I sat on my fanny and bounced down the hill.

"Gus, I love you so much! You're my hero," I said, rubbing him behind the ears as I opened the back door.

"I was getting worried about you," Margaret said. "I'll dry the dogs off. Where's your linen closet?"

"In the hall between the guestrooms. Use the ones on the shelf labeled *Dogs*."

Margaret commented that the puppies were surprisingly warm, and I told her schnauzers have an undercoat of fur that grows close to their bodies and acts like thermal underwear.

"Margaret, would you like some s'mores? I feel like celebrating."

"Yes, I'll build the fire and you get Graham crackers, chocolate, and marshmallows."

That evening as the fire blazed in the hearth, Lucy cuddled on the sofa, wrapped in a soft throw. And perhaps I read her mind when I thought she was unusually grateful to be safe in the house. She had lost some of her innocence. The outdoors that the Gooses loved was filled with peril. But all was well tonight. The family was together. Gus put his head on one of my furry bedroom shoes and stared into the fire.

#

On Christmas Eve, Larkin arrived loaded down with gifts. I got her settled in my newly decorated guestroom. All the boxes had been removed, and I'd painted it a dark forest green and ordered heavy bedding in gold, green, and persimmon. The carved fruitwood bed had belonged to my grandmother Isabel, who had delivered her five children there. My grandmother was Larkin's great aunt. As I pulled the door closed, I suggested that she might enjoy a nap before dinner.

After dinner the three of us gathered around the fireplace in the living room. I read off the times of Christmas services at The Episcopal Church of the Incarnation. It was a beautiful old church with a lively congregation and a priest who was the real thing. I knew that Margaret had lost most of her religious leanings as a teenager. I wasn't surprised when she declined to attend.

Larkin added, "Just tell your friends that I'm your pagan cousin from Georgia. I don't do church."

With bittersweet resignation, I was content to go to the Christmas Eve service alone. After all, I had lived long enough to know a Norman Rockwell Christmas was only an illusion.

Christmas Day arrived with an ice storm that left the bare trees glistening and the evergreens looking like Irish lace. After we exchanged gifts, we had a light breakfast of cranberry scones, Greek yogurt, and hot chocolate. Because the Gooses had been attracted to Rudolf, each received a life-sized puppy from Santa Claus. Having lost much of my mental capabilities during December, I actually wondered whether to give the girl puppy to Lucy or to Gus.

Having spent many years with my family on Christmas Day, I was enjoying this later part of life where my friends were included in the celebration. When Harriet arrived with a fuzzy Manolo Barknik shoe for Gus; J.Jay with a pair of tennis socks for Lucy; and Helen with a bottle of Pouilly-Fuisse, I knew Christmas had finally arrived.

After dinner I got up from the table to make coffee and scanned the breakfront for liqueurs. I gazed out the window. While we were eating, snow had silently fallen. The mountains had been draped in white, not the hard white of the earlier ice storm but soft white of Colorado powder. My guests gathered at the window to see the immense beauty of a Highlands snowstorm.

"What happened to the molding? And the missing sheetrock under the window?" asked Helen, pointing to a hole in the wall.

"The Gooses ate it. You've heard the phrase, *Eaten out of house and home*? Well, there have been times when I wondered if this was happening to me," I said.

"My goodness!" exclaimed J.Jay.

"There don't seem to be enough chew sticks in the world to satiate their habit," I explained.

"You're kidding?" mused Harriet. "Was their mother a beaver?"

"Had to be," I said.

Then I opened the back door. Winnie and Lucy dashed out. We watched as they moved slowly around the yard leaving snow trenches to mark their paths. A few minutes later, Lucy began to hop from spot to spot licking the snow. Gus stood beside me in the foyer and stared at his friends. He decided that the white world was too strange for him to negotiate. He hunched up his back and pooped where he stood.

"Gus Goose!" I cried.

"Ohhh," moaned my guests.

Knowing he was in trouble, Gus charged out the door. I ran for the usual clean-up supplies. Afterwards, I let the dogs inside.

Helen gazed outside and with her natural exuberance said, "You know what this powder is good for?"

"Snow angels!" we replied, charging outside as if we were six years old. We threw ourselves on the snow and moved our arms and legs up and down! A sheer delight!

Afterwards, we sat in the living room and ate plum pudding with brandied hard sauce. The scent of Colombian coffee was so grand that even the non-coffee drinkers had a taste. I let out a long sigh. The little tree had "snowed" on the remaining presents, and the fire had a few smoldering embers. The Gooses slept soundly curled up against Winnie. As I took in this pleasant scene, I knew what really mattered was the friends and family who were here; enough money to pay December's bills; the magnitude of God's love for us and his glorious gift of dogs.

Chapter Ten

Everyone's a Dog Trainer

By January the ten-month-old Gooses had taken possession of my house; it was a home invasion of the canine variety. I belonged to them. They dictated which clothes I wore, which pieces of furniture were covered in dog protective throws, how much money I had left at the end of the month, and so forth and so on. I was amazed that this had happened.

As my situation with the Gooses had become more problematic, my friends came to the rescue—each and every one had become an expert on raising puppies. It was as if the channel surfers had paused long enough to internalize a few rules from Cesar Milan's show, others had read the flyleaf on a bestseller by the monks of New Skete, and all believed with the infallibility of inerrant Bible enthusiasts that their method of training dogs was the only one.

If I was fortunate enough to entertain, the Gooses became the focus of conversation. Like a new mother with a colicky baby, I'd been hoping my dinner party would be a fun-filled diversion from my daily life. My guests—bright, interesting people—were seated in the living room, totally enthralled by two little fur balls with dark, twinkling eyes.

"You don't leave their food down all day, do you?" asked one expert dog trainer.

"No, I leave it down until noon." This was bending one of the rules that every trainer took as fact: "Only leave the puppies' food out for fifteen minutes." The truth was the Gooses ate at noon, rarely any sooner.

"Be sure to take their water bowl up at 5:00 P.M.," instructed another well-meaning trainer.

"Yes, I do that." That rule stated: If your puppy doesn't have water after 5:00 P.M., he will hold his urine until morning. The Gooses hadn't read that book either; they remained oblivious.

"Sit!" screamed another guest-trainer. He held a piece of cheese over Gus's head as an incentive. Gus sat.

"I don't allow the Gooses to eat people food. Their stomachs are smaller than my fist. Any change in their diet is followed by a bout of diarrhea. That makes house-training, which at the moment is challenging, impossible."

"Isabel, do you shout at them and really get angry when they potty in the house?" asked yet another guest-trainer.

"I don't shout."

"You should lower your voice an octave when you speak to them."

"Lucy, down!" yelled a guest-trainer when Lucy Goose jumped on the sofa.

"The word *down* is used when they jump up on people. *Off* is the correct command when they hop up on the furniture."

I'd tried to train the Gooses. Gus sat and stayed when told to do so; Lucy looked at me and *rooed* as if she were saying, "You don't really want me to become one of those trained dogs, do you?" And I thought it an abhorrent situation to witness a female under the command of anyone.

What I learned from this confrontation was that the ratio of four guest-trainers to two puppies was more effective. I also knew my friends couldn't keep up the intensity of this lesson for long. For my guests, the Gooses were grandchildren who'd come for a delightful afternoon visit, and later, would go home with their parents.

More importantly, I'd decided that for every golden rule of dog training there was a codicil that no one admits—not the vet, not other dog owners, not even the trainers. We, the defenseless amateurs, have to learn it for ourselves.

For example, Gus had realized that when he was in the pen, he could stand up and aim outside, then sprinkle the kitchen floor without any ill effects to his living space. His crate stood in the center of the kitchen; if he had been a garden sprinkler, he could have watered every square-foot of floor. Lucy, before eliminating in the pen, would bark and scratch the floor, creating a horrendous racket that woke me up around 3:00 A.M. If I let her out, I'd be reinforcing her barking in the crate—something my quiet schnauzers rarely did. If I let her poop, there would be a nasty mess to clean up in the morning. I'd learned by trial and error that when she scratches the floor of her pen during the night, it was best to take her out.

Lucy had learned that if she rubbed her nose, I gave her a Benadryl in a chicken-flavored Pill Pocket, thinking her allergies were bothering her. She liked the taste of a Pill Pocket more than her daily kibble. In her mind it was a treat. So Lucy greeted me in the morning with an Academy Award rendition of "Oh, My Nose! I Can't Breathe!" She'd rub her nose with her paws then scoot around my bed nose first. She was waiting for me to say, "Is your nose bothering you? Do you want a pill?" She keyed in on the words *nose, want,* and *pill.* The longer the performance lasted, the more demonstrative she became. One morning she sat down in front of me and hit her nose with one front paw and then the other! As she goes through her performance, she'll pause and look at me. Translation: "Have you finally understood? I need a Pill Pocket!" I never know anymore when her allergies are bothering her because she wants a Pill Pocket all the time. But the performance is quite extraordinary.

#

"You don't know me, but I've heard you could use some help with your schnauzer puppies."

"Ya think?" I said into the phone. "It's very kind of you to call. I thought they would be easier. I'm sinking. They've taken over . . . they eat houses . . . some friends have wondered if they were a cross breed of beavers and schnauzers."

Not only did my friends turn into dog trainers, but they, along with perfect strangers like the kind woman on the phone, were going to tell me the good news—a dog training class was being formed. It would meet on Sunday afternoons.

When Nell mentioned that she had signed her dog up for the same class, I wondered why Betty Beau—that ideal specimen of the canine world—needed to be trained. I asked a mutual friend, "What has Betty Beau been doing that has upset Nell?"

She answered in a very Southern drawl, "Recently, at a par-ty Betty Beau pranced around the liv-in' room, pee-in' in all the guests' poc-ket-books."

I decided to take Lucy to the obedience classes because she was the more docile of the two. I was hoping that what she learned I could later teach Gus. I missed the first lesson because I couldn't find the location, a beautiful old homestead dating back to the 1800s with a sign that was visible only to those with a pair of binoculars. As instructed, I went to the second class prepared with a choker collar ordered from Drs. Foster and Smith's catalog. Being a Type A Personality, I was perturbed that I had to wait thirty minutes for the rest of the class to purchase the same equipment from the instructor. Meanwhile Lucy, intimidated by all the big dogs, tried to claw her way up my body and into my arms like a toddler at pre-school. When she tired of climbing, she sat on the ground and wrapped her front legs around my knee. She looked like a monkey. I looked like a fool.

When the class began, Lucy did better with the exercises than I'd expected. My homework was to teach her to walk in a triangle, stopping at the vertices. I wondered how this would transfer into potty training. Perhaps the best I could hope for was the classes would promote me to the alpha dog status that I now craved.

My birthday was the following week; I was turning sixty. I planned to celebrate both in my hometown of Atlanta and in Highlands. The next Sunday I fixed lunch for my closest friends here and missed the third class. The following Sunday it snowed and this Southern Belle became an official dog-training-class dropout.

#

Soon thereafter, I had lunch with Kathie who was on the board of the Cashiers-Highlands Humane Society, an outstanding facility. She, too, had heard that I was having problems with the Gooses. She suggested that I call the Society's dog behaviorist for help. Dr. Heide Coppotelli, touted as a Master Dog Trainer, had worked with numerous shelter dogs that had a vast variety of problems. I considered Dr. Coppotelli to be an excellent recommendation and agreed to call her.

During my phone conversation with Dr. Coppotelli, I learned her Ph.D. was in psychology. Human psychology. She had been born in northern Germany, grew up in Chicago, and married an Italian. She sounded like a gentle soul who'd put the boot camp philosophy of raising dogs aside for a more humane approach.

"If you think of my puppies as little French children, you'll have a leg up on understanding them. *Au naturale. A la Rousseau.*"

She laughed and promised to e-mail me the directions to her house. She ended our conversation with, "This isn't an emergency situation. Let's meet next Tuesday at 2:00 P.M."

I agreed. She had brought my anxiety level down a notch by saying my situation wasn't an emergency, whether it was or not. I could relate to the information she sent via emails, especially the part that said some small dogs have an extraordinary proclivity to chew and chew and chew.

Our trip to Dr. Coppotelli's would take forty-five minutes, driving east on Route 64 then north to the Lake Toxaway area. I cleaned out the car and then tossed in my doggy-diaper bag. Because Gus got carsick more often than Lucy, I put him in the front seat.

When I went into the house to get Lucy, Gus set off the car alarm. In the six years I'd owned the Honda, this had never happened. Because the car was in the garage, the nerve-wrenching sound of the alarm was intensified to a painful pitch. I darted into the garage and grabbed the door handle in an attempt to free Gus. The door was locked! Gus looked up at me with a terrified expression on his face. I tried the door handle again as Gus's little black eyes pleaded with me.

"Hang in there, Gus. I'll be right back."

I charged into the house and got my car keys, trying to remember whether the keypad had a button that would turn the alarm off. Then I ran into the garage and aimed it at the car and pressed down.

Silence! Gus looked grateful.

"I don't know what you did but it's over," I told him.

But he gave me that look of his with the whites of his eyes showing that said, "Why did you do that to me? I'm plotting revenge!"

I loaded Lucy into the car and crept down the steep driveway. I reached down into my purse and pulled out the directions. After we drove through the switchbacks Dr. Coppotelli had described, I noticed Gus was standing up. This was never a good sign. My first thought was he might jump into my lap and cause me to veer to the right, dropping off the mountain or if I veered to the left, I'd be steering into oncoming traffic. But jumping wasn't on Gus's mind.

I glanced over at him again. His sides were moving in and out like billows. His neck extended down like a horse drinking from a trough. His mouth opened and out came half a gallon of orange-colored liquid, pouring into my pocketbook.

"Oh, Gus!" I patted his head and he sat down. He had aimed well; almost everything he threw up was in my purse.

We stopped for roadwork and the guy directing traffic waved to Gus. He was the epitome of a cute puppy and rarely did he go unnoticed.

"Would you like to have him?" I screamed out the window. The man smiled and motioned us on.

In these mountains during the winter months there's rarely an occupied house or opened business to rescue me if I get lost. I made mental notes of landmarks so I could reverse the directions and get home safely. When I turned into Dr. Coppotelli's neighborhood, I spotted the bright green roof on her log cabin that she'd described, and pulled to a stop under a grove of pine trees. A woman, who I assumed was she, rounded up six German shepherds and put them inside her house.

I got out my doggie-diaper bag, and cleaned Gus and wiped the seat off. I grabbed a pen from a small overhead compartment and my notebook from the backseat.

"Hi, I'm Isabel. You must be Dr. Coppotelli."

"Please call me Heide. Come on inside but leave the puppies in the car."

I couldn't help think: Had someone warned her? I entered her house while the shepherds barked at me, arousing my anxiety. I was frightened of Heide's rescued pack. She instructed them to stop barking and they did. Then she said, "Set-tle," while moving her hand in a circle as if she was mixing cake batter. The dogs became relaxed and at ease. They were no longer in an alert, watchful state of mind. It had been months since I had seen the Gooses relaxed. Instead, they lounged like a couple of sentries on duty. The slightest sound caused them to bark ferociously.

Heidi said, "You may bring the puppies inside now."

I thought the shepherds might attack them, but when my dogs pattered over to make friends, they remained settled. The Gooses sniffed them, wanting to play with them. But the shepherds remained settled.

"I'm impressed. I can see how useful this command can be," I said. "It's a new one for me,"

"Please sit down," Heidi said, motioning to an Adirondack chair with a floral cushion.

I sat down and took out my notebook, getting ready for her lecture. As she spoke, I had a feeling I'd arrived in doggie nirvana. Her home was filled with peace and quiet. This was a stark contrast to my life with the Gooses. Last night I had cleared my throat and the dogs went ballistic. If the doorbell rang and the bloodhound came on TV to help the cat find its litter box, the puppies went berserk. If Gus burst out with ferocious barking, Lucy—not knowing what had caused his attack-demeanor—followed suit. Their abrupt, high-pitched barking caused me to jump with fear, a symptom of my lingering post-traumatic stress disorder.

Now in doggie nirvana, the Gooses walked over to a wicker basket filled with toys and pulled one out to play with it. This surprised me because at home they refused to take a toy out of their wicker basket. Thankfully, the German shepherds remained settled. I relaxed. When the hour was over, I didn't want to leave.

During the time with Heide, the leader of her pack, a white shepherd, stood up and barked casually at a dog across the street. Heide turned to her and said, "Yes, Gretchen, I see that dog. Thank you for telling me." Then she gave the hand signal for the settle command. Gretchen stopped barking and lay down.

According to Heide, training dogs is all about the connection one has with her dogs. If one of the Gooses wanted my attention at a time when I couldn't give it or didn't want to, I was to caress his cheek for seven seconds. She said that all dogs loved this. She called Lucy over. As Heide rubbed, Lucy smiled.

I had an intense connection with Gus. He was so smart that he had trained me to understand his behavior and anticipate his needs. I knew he felt this connection, too. Except for not always coming when he was called, he rarely disobeyed. Lucy, on the other hand, was more laid back and therefore had less demonstrative behavior to understand, relate to, and correct. Recently, Gus had become the alpha dog. After that occurred, her personality changed. She appeared to be an angry subservient dog. In the mornings Lucy barked at me as I came into the kitchen to let the Gooses out. Her greeting seemed to say, "Intruder! Intruder! Intruder!" in a tone similar to a computer-generated voice. I had finally concluded she didn't like me. This made me feel sad and frustrated. That was our relationship. It was similar to the cat owner who said, "I'm just her can opener."

Before leaving doggy nirvana, I asked about the beautiful leather leashes that were hanging by Heide's door. They were extra long with brass fittings. She explained that a dog owner could achieve subtle sensitivity by using a leather leash in much the same way a horseback rider uses his legs to communicate with the horse in dressage.

The leashes reminded me of the tack my daughter Margaret cared for when she was only six years old. She cleaned it on Friday night preparing for a Saturday horse show. The scent of Murphy's Oil Soap reminds me of those years. I decided to buy two leashes from Heide. Each time I'd take them off the coat rack, I'd think of Margaret and what she might be doing with her horseback-riding students.

Looking back on my visit with Heide, I realized that by osmosis I had absorbed more about dog training than I had from any other source. Yes, in the middle of doggie chaos, this was my first contact with a style of disciplinary training that I could easily fit into my life. I could use the techniques when they were needed not as a separate training session. I could go home and throw away the whip and chains!

Chapter Eleven
Bridge Work

When February arrived, the eleven-month-old puppies could be located easily in the barren landscape with a sweeping glance out the back door or from the front deck. When someone asked if the puppies were good company during this lonely time of year, I replied that good company doesn't go potty in the living room. In fact, it seemed the puppies and I were on opposing teams playing a game of co-habitation. Even implementing Hiedi's training didn't appear to break the bond of my littermates. They were hyper-focused on each other and I remained an adjunct.

It was the bleakest part of mid-winter; many of my friends had retreated to warmer climates. I missed my Buckhead friends, the ones who really knew me, as well as being homesick for Atlanta. I had grown up with the city. In order to move to Highlands, I'd suppressed my love for living there, truncated my feelings for friends, and professed my fill of Atlanta's arts scene. But home would always be that city of green and the refined, well-educated people who live there.

As I was returning from a day-trip to Atlanta, my spirits soared when I rounded a curve on Route 441 and saw the mountains for the first time. They held the promise of peace and security. And a wealth of newfound friends who loved the arts and learning as much as I did. The Scottish stronghold of Highlands was unfolding before me, awakening new and forgotten interests.

On the final leg of my journey, I made a right-hand turn onto Route 246, which began the drive up the mountain to Highlands. Turning onto that road, I exhaled. Time slowed down to mountain time. I smiled as I drove by an old Sinclair gas station sign with a green dinosaur; in a few minutes, an old Pure sign with blue rick-rack around the edge would come into view. The protective cloak I had clung to in the city of nearly six million fell away and I breathed deeply.

Thirty minutes into the drive, I saw Dusty's on the side of the road. Dusty's is a small, family-owned grocery that caters to the weekend trade who like heat-and-eat gourmet items and prime cuts of meat and fresh seafood. My favorite is their old-fashioned caramel layer cakes. As I drove into the parking lot, I was surprised to see Mr. Peters's red pickup with its license plate proclaiming his love for wildlife, the same wildlife he hunted, killed, and later ate. But that was the kind of hunting I could respect: Kill a bear, feed your family.

I pulled my winter jacket tightly around me as I got out of the car. The February cold was as brutal as the landscape was bare. And yet, I had grown to find beauty in our winters— the peaceful color of gray-green rocks and trees covered with lichen. Gnarled tree branches were backed by the evergreens resembling a hand-painted Japanese screen. When I first saw the lichen, I remembered my high school biology. It was an organism comprised of fungus and algae growing together in symbiosis. Hopefully, the residents of the Highlands Plateau can interface with the delicate eco-system in a similar manner.

"Howdy, Miz A.," said the Peters clan. "Are you returnin' from Atlanta?"

"Yes, I am. I don't want to hear any more jokes about it being Sodom and Gomorrah rolled into one. I'm a little tired today."

"We're here buyin' hot dogs for the weekend. Expectin' some relatives from Florida."

"Well, just let me know if you'd like the Gooses to come over and entertain them."

"Is them dogs house-trained yet?"

"No one has a perfect dog," I said, laughing.

I bought some currant scones and white tea for tomorrow's breakfast. I, too, was expecting house guests. As a hostess, I liked to create the feeling that they'd arrived in Scotland. Tartan plaid throws, thistles on the dinnerware, bagpipe music in the background.

Before leaving for Atlanta I had left my door unlocked in case the Woodfins arrived before I got home. When I pulled into the driveway, I saw Christie and her daughter Cutler were playing with the puppies on the front deck. Christie is a tall, sleek beauty. An educational consultant, who places students in the best schools and colleges for them. Cutler, tall like her mom, adorable, and exuding personality, had loved animals since her childhood and now worked for a veterinarian. I confessed that the puppies weren't completely house-trained and that about once a month Lucy urinates in the house and Gus has to be watched closely at 5:00 P.M.

Cutler suggested, "You should use the crate training method more consistently. You need to get another pen. So that each dog will have his own space to keep clean. And don't give up. I'm sure they'll catch on," Cutler continued.

"Okay. I'll do that. I appreciate the advice."

"You're dealing with two problems—first, house-training the puppies and second, Lucy has a condition known as *submissive urination*. She tinkles as a sign of submission to any stranger who reaches down to pat her," Cutler said.

"And when that happens, my guests turn to me and shout, 'Isabel, there's urine on the floor!' 'Oh, no!' I yell, pretending to be surprised."

"Lucy will probably outgrow this unpleasant form of greeting. Most puppies do."

"Which of the Gooses do you like best?" asked Christie, sensing there was no more to be said about potty training.

"I'd have to think about that. I don't have a ready answer."

They were so different, presented different challenges. Were endearing in different ways. We'd lived together for almost a year. The Gooses had become an intricate part of my life. When I came home on a dark winter's evening, I knew they would be waiting to greet me. Two warm bodies squealing and dancing around.

"As I love each of the puppies' endearing traits, I love that dog."

"Tell me more," Christie said.

"I think it is the way you love your children . . . when you have more than one. I love them equally but differently."

Gus was always in motion and getting into trouble, which made him the more difficult of the two. He chased bugs and bit at flies—all boy. He came to me when his stomach was upset and laid across my thighs for warmth and healing. At other times, Gus was my protector in a way that neither of my husbands had been. I loved that quality! Also, Gus was a polite gentleman who always waited to be asked onto my big bed. He liked to have his paw held. He would sit in front of me and hold out his paw. I would massage it gently, imagining his eyes rolling back in his head.

Like the winners of the Westminster Dog Show, Gus had a visible spirit. When he entered a room, he was Jay Leno taking the stage, "Here I am. Play with me and have a good time!" Gus had a combination of qualities that made people love him. He was Peter Rabbit, naughty but adorable. Gus was Wilbur in *Charlotte's Web*, innocent and free. He was Mumbles in the movie *Happy Feet*, a unique underdog that had triumphed over his own fears.

Why I loved Gus was the same reason I'd loved the men in my life. They were interesting. They were smart. They were endearing and tender. When I had a piece of their heart, I knew that I had something that wasn't often shared. That, in itself, was special.

Lucy was truly a beautiful dog. Her black eyelashes rose to meet her brows that stood up forming plumes like peacock feathers. She had a snow-white triangle of curly fur on her chest and similar markings on her butt. The fur on her legs looked like lamb's fur. She was a picture of beauty when she lounged on a snow bank in the backyard as if to say, "I'm at home in the cold mountains."

Lucy Goose was more of a social being that still needed reassurance after I'd gotten angry with her. She still sat with her fanny on the sofa and her head on my rib cage just like she did the day we met. She was the sweeter of the two puppies and would accept my affection for longer periods of time. Gus became restless. When he walked away he seemed to be saying, "I'm a guy and can take only so much of this cuddling."

I'd read about the spirit of the schnauzer breed and had come to be a great admirer. I marveled as the puppies charged out the door to go potty when the steps were covered with ice. If they slipped, they bounced right back up and went on their way. The freezing-cold weather, deep snow, and briar bushes didn't slow them down. Gus had found Lucy in eye-blinding sleet and never made a wrong turn. The Gooses would take on any animal or person who threatened my safety—regardless of size or scent. When they sat next to me inside, they positioned themselves facing the door ready to confront an intruder.

When the Woodfins left, I was so sad. It had been lovely being with friends from Atlanta, especially in the winter when most equate a visit to Highlands as traveling to Antarctica. They'd come to Highlands to be sure I was all right. They had met the Gooses and given sound advice I needed to hear. But Christie and Cutler were more than friends, they were family. The house had been blessed as if an Episcopal priest had stood by the hearth and made the sign of the cross. And the bridge back to Atlanta strengthened.

Chapter Twelve
Spring on the Horizon

Winter in the Appalachian Mountains was ending. Yet snow was still a possibility until the middle of May. I'd seen freezing temperatures wilt the emerging hostas and early grasses. Consequently, the month of March was much more like winter than springtime. I longed for the end of March when the jonquils and forsythia bring the welcome color of yellow to the gray landscape, and the flowering trees begin to bloom white, pink, and burgundy.

For my little family of three, March marked the schnauzers' first birthday. We'd survived a year! A year that had turned out to be so different from what I'd imagined. Not only had the schnauzers refused to fall into my life like good little soldiers marching along, they had taken over my house and run off with my heart.

Gus weighed twenty-three pounds. His coat was a gorgeous gunmetal gray. Lucy weighed almost thirty pounds. She was a true salt-and-pepper schnauzer, looking much like she had the day we met.

I was wondering what to do to celebrate their first birthday. I thought it would be fun to invite all my friends who owned schnauzers to come to a party. But the Gooses weren't socialized beings. As they were growing up, no one wanted to host two not-completely house-trained schnauzers. If I took them out in public, they assumed an attacking posture that frightened everyone, including me. As for being a good host and hostess, the puppies were more home protectors. Welcoming guests and sharing weren't their strong suits.

I was surprised when the parents of one of their littermates called and asked if we'd participate in a birthday reunion; they referred to it as a "play-date." They had seen a story of mine about the puppies in *The Mountain Laurel* magazine. They were the proud parents of Bailey and said that another set of parents lived on their street at Highlands Falls Country Club. We decided to meet near the clubhouse for a reunion and afterwards let the dogs run on the empty golf course.

Bundled in parkas, scarves, and gloves, we proud parents stood on the wheat-colored grass to watch our dogs become re-acquainted. The question in all our minds was: Would the puppies remember their siblings? They greeted each other with only a few sniffs and immediately began to play so we concluded that they did. I thought the brothers would be immaculately groomed in the traditional schnauzer cut, but they had more of a poodle-puppy cut like the Gooses. Bailey was salt and pepper; Teddy was almost solid white. Lucy was the biggest and longest. After a few runs around the golf course, she stood by me while Gus ran laps with his brothers. Film and photos were taken to commemorate the event.

When I asked about potty training, the parents told me that their dogs were trained when they got them at three months of age. Why, of course, they could go all night without an accident.

"*Really?*" I said, looking down at mine.

#

In mid-March I went to Raleigh with my friends Nell and Anne to see the "Monet in Normandy" exhibit at the North Carolina Museum of Art. There were familiar paintings of the light effects on Rouen Cathedral and several of the grain stacks. Many were painted in Monet's garden at Giverny. But the most exciting paintings were the ones from private collections—the Monet's I'd not seen in books. My favorite Monet is *The Magpie*, a sun filled snow-scape with a solitary bird. The Normandy exhibit introduced me to *Frost*, a painting of bare bushes wearing windblown snow; Monet's circular brushwork captured the wind. *Snow Effect at Giverny* had been painted in soft violets and shades of white. Viewing those beautiful paintings renewed my creative spirit, my life's blood.

Before leaving Highlands I had taken the Gooses to board with their breeder, Sadie. She and her family would be leaving town on Sunday so when I returned to pick them up, they'd be in the chicken coop attached to the lower level of the house. When I'd learned Sadie planned to leave them outside, the following thought flashed through my mind: They don't have any clothes! Then I'd told myself to get a grip—they were dogs.

Sunday had been a cold day in Raleigh and would be even colder in the mountains. On our return trip we'd driven eight hours crossing North Carolina. I thought the journey would never end as we wound our way over one mountain and down the next in the true blackness one sees when miles from city lights. The cold, the all-encompassing blackness, and the feeling of being alone were so acute that it heightened one's senses. Knowing the isolated location and hilly terrain of Sadie's house, Nell and Anne refused to let me go alone. What if I fell? What if I needed to call for help? I was known to be extremely independent, but I acquiesced.

We turned off the highway onto Route 107. Nell spotted the school bus sign that signaled a left turn onto Sadie's street. We bounced along potholes sprinkled with gravel. I hit the gas pedal and sent us over the blind hill into the thick darkness of the sky. I turned quickly into Sadie's driveway and parked in the slot used for her husband's truck.

"I'll turn the headlights on while you search for the Gooses," Nell said, as she climbed into the driver's seat.

I'd brought my best flashlight and packed it where it was easily accessible. I turned it on and walked in the direction of the house. I heard the sound of growling dogs guarding their homestead; the enraged barking sounded like hundreds of dogs. As I hiked up the hillside in bitter cold, I could see only a few steps ahead as the flashlight beam bounced along. A small beagle began to encircle me; I'd seen him there before. I focused on my mission. All I had to do was climb the hill and I'd run into the lower level of the house, locate the chicken coop—I'd never seen one in my life—and rescue the Gooses.

Suddenly, in the background noise I heard a growling sound that modulated like a cat purring. As I've said, there are bobcats and mountain lions in the area. Both were expert hunters. Bobcats have been known to kill house cats and attack dogs as large as chows, leaving fang marks in their skulls. They have binocular vision that makes them highly effective night hunters. Both wildcats stalk their prey then leap to attack the base of its skull. Both have strong jaws and long teeth; both can kill with one powerful bite through the spinal cord. If the purring was coming from a bobcat, the puppies were in danger. If it was a mountain lion, I was the probable target.

"Gus, Gus?" I called, thinking that he would answer. Thinking that he was a guy who would help me find them. But all I could hear was the growling dogs. As I got closer to the house, the noises became more directional. Listening carefully, I knew that Sadie's schnauzers were on the left side of the upper deck. The beagle was winding in and out where I expected to find the chicken coop. As the dogs quieted down, I thought I heard Gus's bark. Then came Lucy's characteristic *roo-roo*.

I walked along on level ground next to the basement until I saw two small dogs. They were pawing the door of the chicken coop, running their nails across the wire and making a terrible noise. I shined the flashlight on them. They looked odd so I stooped down to see them face to face; they were a light gray color but clearly Gus and Lucy. I looked on the gate for their leashes but didn't find them. When I cracked the gate open, the dogs ran out.

As we began jogging down the hill, the Gooses jumped up and put their paws on my seat. That nearly threw me off balance, but each time I caught myself before I fell. I was too worried about the growling wildcat to slow down and discipline them. I could only hope that the puppies and I were moving further away from that animal with each step we took. When I began walking down the mountain, I realized that I may have turned my back on a mountain lion. I knew doing that told him: "I'm prey. Come get me."

The puppies were still with me and unharmed. The schnauzers on the deck continued to bark, the beagle encircled us in a protective way, and the purring came closer. My heart beat faster. We *were* being stalked.

I could see the car. I was relieved to hear the engine running and see the backdoor was open. I knew every second counted. But to my great surprise, the Gooses were reluctant to jump in Nell's car! I caught Gus and tossed him on the backseat. He quickly turned to face me.

"Stay!" I said, as I put my hand up in a signal that I knew he'd obey.

Gus froze.

I thought Lucy would follow Gus into the car but she refused.

"Lucy, get in the car!" As I leaned over to pick her up, she ran a few feet up the hillside.

"Lucy, come here," I said softly. She retreated a few more feet but I caught her and jumped in the car, slamming the door behind us. As Nell turned the car towards the house, we saw a small tan cat that probably weighed ten to fifteen pounds.

"Do you see that? The blue eyes." We all spoke at once.

"I think it's a mountain lion cub," Anne said. "I've heard the locals talk about their electric-blue eyes. "

"It's a gorgeous animal!" I said.

The dogs were shivering from the cold; I rubbed them and held them close for warmth. Anne offered to hold one but I couldn't let go of either dog. In that moment, I felt more attached to them than ever before. I hugged and kissed them in possessive maternal way. Anne commented that they smelled like smoke, which accounted for their light gray color. They were covered in ashes that I quickly brushed off. Nell drove back to the main road and then dropped us at home.

That night the dogs slept with me in the big bed. They didn't act like Mexican jumping beans as they had in the past when I'd tried for a threesome. Gus lay on my left and Lucy on my right, stretched out like two lifeless sausages. We were so tired from our weekend adventures that none of us moved until the morning sunlight hit the apricot walls of my bedroom, making a picture that Monet might have enjoyed painting—*Light Effect in a Highlands Bedroom*.

#

Although I'd taught elementary school for almost twenty years, my teaching profession had begun as a means of putting my first husband, Kerry Clayton, through Harvard Business School. After our divorce, teaching became a way of supporting my four-year old daughter and me. However, I was an artist by nature, a totally right-brained being. I loved the creative process. I loved the thought of having created a painting or a book that would outlive me. When I was with other artists, there was easy communication, a seamless soul-to-soul exchange.

At a party I met the renowned portrait painter Comer Jennings. I was excited to meet him because he had lived in my grandmother Isabel's house on Woodward Way in Buckhead, a beautiful old English Tudor set on a wooded lot. I told Comer that during my childhood I had loved to visit my grandmother. I had played mah-jongg on the upstairs landing and picked jonquils in the front yard. I knew where the secret panel was in the foyer.

I thought that Comer and I might bond over our love of painting. So I mentioned that I had studied with Alice Williams and Marc Chatov, who were also well-known artists and portrait painters in Atlanta. We had an enjoyable conversation. Then I mentioned, "I heard you have a puppy."

"Yes, I did. I gave him away this morning; he was a six-month-old Scotty. All I did was clean up after him. I couldn't get any work done. You know, people want their portraits done yesterday."

"Yes, I do. I've painted portraits of children although my talent isn't in the same class as yours." I'd been surprised that it had taken several months for Hong Men Zou to copy my grandmother Isabel's portrait. Yet, when Mr. Hong brought it to me, I felt as if she had come back to life, the image was that good.

"I have two schnauzers about a year old. They've been a handful."

"I bet that I can match you story for story!" Comer said.

Never being one to shirk from a challenge, I said, "Last week I walked into the kitchen and noticed that they were devouring the foam in their dog bed. I assumed that the zipper had come open and one of the dogs had put his nose in and enlarged the opening until both schnauzers could lie side by side, pulling out chunks of foam. I was so tired of cleaning up after them that I just tossed the bed over the dog gate into the living room.

"Later, I made sure to close the zipper and returned the bed to them. The next morning the Gooses were covered in foam rubber. They had shredded the inner cushion into thousands of tiny bits. I imagine one of them had learned to grab the zipper tab, then jerk his head around until it opened. Frankly, I was surprised that they hadn't choked on all that foam.

"The next day Gus unzipped the pillows on the living room sofa and shredded the foam. That evening while he was watching TV with me, he noticed the drawstrings on my jeans; he found them a delight to chew and quickly untied the knotted ends. Then he noticed the zipper on my pants and cagily went for it.

'Oh, no! Don't even think about it,' I yelled. Gus learned that all the pants I wore had a zipper in front. At times, my zipper would attract him. He'd jump up and try to catch the tab in his mouth—I guess that was what he was doing. If he'd unzipped my jeans, I'm certain he expected to find foam!"

At the party Comer said my story won first prize. He couldn't beat it. I went on to tell him that my dogs had become a source of wonderful stories. In fact, I was writing a book about them.

"It can't *possibly* be worth it!" Comer exclaimed, in a dramatic manner only an artist can do well.

#

I loved my dogs, but hated seeing the house I'd worked so hard on trashed and soiled. I rationalized their destruction better than their soiling. When I was going out, I'd get dressed and shout *Down!* as I made my way through their kitchen and out the door, hoping to be untouched by dirty paws and to emerge wearing clothes un-snagged by doggy claws. One evening I noticed the corner of a kitchen cabinet had been chewed beyond recognition! How can I repair that?

"You two aren't worth it! I can't take much more of this! Do you hear me?" I screamed as I left their kitchen. It had been over a decade since I'd lost my temper.

Chapter Thirteen
Landscaping on the Cheap

Because the Highlands Plateau is classified as a rainforest, during the previous summer it had been difficult to keep the Gooses out of the mud and the mud out of the house. More quickly than I had thought possible, the puppies had eradicated the grass as they created bare pathways in and out of the woods and around the backyard. So I decided to do a little landscaping before summer arrived. Respecting the eco-system, I wanted to change the yard as little as possible. My plan began with a phone order to Home Depot for fifty bags of bark chips, ten bags of pea gravel, and an outdoor dog pen.

It was a lovely April morning. The sky was Carolina blue again, the temperature 60 degrees. I had dressed in my spring-summer uniform, a t-shirt and jeans. My silver hair was blowing in the breeze as I stood with a mug of coffee on the front deck reading our newspaper, *The Highlander,* and awaiting the Home Depot delivery.

Earlier that morning, I'd had Lucy leashed and ready to go out the door. Because she was still frightened of doors, she hesitated. This was the moment Gus had anticipated. With the ease of a jackrabbit, he leaped over her. Free once again in the great outdoors. On most occasions, he circled the yard and quickly returned. However, today he was working out excess energy with one of his romps around the neighborhood. His little mind seemed to shout, "Faster! Forward! Up that hill and down the next." He was totally absorbed in his runner's high when I'd called to him.

I heard the Home Depot truck grinding its gears as it maneuvered the tight turns through the woods. I put my coffee mug on the front deck railing, charged out the back door, and ran to the bottom of the driveway. To my left I saw Gus heading towards Route 64; to my right I heard the truck coming closer. I knew that at any moment Gus might take a shortcut through the woods and run up the driveway. In the middle is a blind curve where one has to hit the accelerator and hope that no one's walking down.

I stood resolutely at the end of the driveway, holding Gus's leash. The driver saw me, and the truck screeched to a halt.

"I'm your next delivery—Allen. My dog's run away."

"I'll be glad to help you look for him. What's his name?" the truck driver asked.

"Gus."

We went in different directions calling for him. I spotted him running in circles in the Peters's backyard. He was leaning into the curves like a speed skater. Mr. Peters was poised against his back door frame.

"What the hell? . . . Does Gus think him's Little Black Sambo?" Mr. Peters shouted.

"I don't think Gus knows that story. It probably just feels good to run in circles. He only does this when he's really happy! He must like you a lot."

Mr. Peters cracked a smile.

"Have I told you—this week—how strange I think 'em dogs is?"

"Not this week. But it may surprise you to know I'm beginning to agree with you. These schnauzers aren't like any dogs I've owned."

When I began to talk with Mr. Peters, the deliveryman knew that I'd found Gus and joined us. Gus was leery of him. So I stepped into Gus's circle and asked the Home Depot driver to stand back. In a taunting manner Gus flew by me a few more times. During the fourth fly-by, he came close enough for me to catch him and attach his leash.

"Got you, Gus Goose!" Then I turned to Mr. Peters and called, "Always good to see you."

As we began walking home, the truck driver asked, "Can I walk him?"

"Sure." I gave him Gus's leash.

"Is he full-grown?"

"Yes. Thirteen months old."

"He's much stronger than he looks," He adjusted his hold on the leash.

"I agree."

The truck driver, thinking about the dog pen on the truck, said, "Mr. Gus, I've got somethin' *real special* for you!"

I laughed. It tickled me that people recognized Gus's spirit and strong personality; they always called him Mr. Gus.

Because I had placed my order by phone, I was amazed at the volume of 50 bags of bark chips. Chalk it up to woman's intuition, it proved to be the right amount to cover my little backyard. The bags of pea gravel would resurface the path from the driveway to the back door. But my real surprise came when the driver took the dog pen off the truck. Each of its four sides measured ten feet long and six feet high. Picturing Gus and Lucy in the pen, I looked down at Gus—now a full 12 inches tall—and laughed. Definitely, overkill.

The deliveryman put the fence at the far end of the yard, all four sides propped up against the house. I felt the joy of having trapped the Gooses in their Cadillac of a dog pen. I was elated, having won this round for co-existence.

The deliveryman glanced over at Gus and then back at the pen.

"That oughta hold Mr. Gus as long as he doesn't dig out!" he shouted.

"Dig out? Oh, dear."

#

The next day my friend Kitty arrived from Atlanta. She has a warm personality that attracts people; I think of her as a "people collector." She's a brunette with a flawless complexion and engaging blue eyes. A Presbyterian minister, an art critic, and an oil painter. Later in life, she had entered Columbia Seminary with a long-range goal of ministering to the city's Latino population. She is fluent in Spanish. To help me with my landscaping project executed by Mexicans, she'd looked up the words for *bark chips*, *pea gravel*, and *dog pen*.

After a late night of theological discussions, Kitty and I got up early and drove ten minutes to the Exxon Station in Cashiers where we were planning to hire three Mexican day laborers. On the way there Kitty said, "I've helped other friends in Atlanta, who wanted to use Mexicans for some carpentry work. They did a beautiful job." Kitty continued, "I know how to do this. When we get to the gas station, pull up to the pumps as if you're going to get gas. I'll get out and quickly get some men. Whatever you do, don't wave money at the crowd! That'll cause a stampede."

I had a knot in my stomach. Even with Kitty there, picking up strangers made me feel uneasy. But I promised to do as I was told. A stampede would certainly start the day on a sour note. A few minutes later, I pulled up to the pumps. Kitty hopped out and returned with Roberto who was probably in his late teens, Rolando, and Armando. By the time we arrived home, we knew the guys had lived here for two years and were originally from a nice suburb of Mexico City. They knew that I had two dogs and needed help landscaping the backyard in order to make dog ownership doable.

We started in the far corner of the yard where the dog pen was; the men erected it in about five minutes. They suggested putting rocks around the outside as a reinforcement against the Gooses digging out. The old sandbox was emptied and placed in the side yard.

"Do you have any yard tools?" the Mexicans asked.

I produced a snow shovel that caused much laughter, a regular shovel, and a rake. Although I didn't have a wheelbarrow, the men were able to carry a bag of bark chips with ease. They raked over the weeds with a shovel and then put the chips down. They took up the tiles at the bottom of the porch steps and relayed them properly—a job that Kitty explained was part of their Spanish heritage.

Pine bark now covered the backyard. The pathway from the drive to the back door had been resurfaced in pea gravel that matched the tiles at the bottom of the back porch steps. I was extremely pleased with the work the men had done. But there were still bushes to plant when Kitty excused herself to take a nap. Now I was alone and had to rely on hand motions and a smattering of French. Even so, in short order three small rhododendron bushes were planted in the bed next to the back porch. The men tried to plant a dark green cypress tree with limbs that twisted and turned like the fans of a dancing Geisha between the garage and the pea gravel path. Young Roberto remarked, "*Piedras. Muchas piedras!*" as he struck the shovel on rock. After a few more shallow holes were dug, it was decided that nothing could be planted there. I wondered if I could return the plants to the nursery, but decided to keep the Mexicans engaged. I convinced Armando, who knew the size to which the cypress would grow, to plant it at the backdoor away from the eaves of the house.

In the delineated beds beside the garage the men were able to plant two yellow cedar bushes, but only two because of the *piedras*. Between the two bushes I decided to put a trellis for morning glories. My last item was a Carolina blue spruce that would grow to be 30 feet high and 12 feet wide. It was the most winsome of trees, and I could hardly wait to paint it covered in snow. The men planted it on the edge of the woods.

When Kitty woke up, she asked how everything had turned out, I said, "*Muchas piedras*. After all, I do live in the mountains."

On our way back to Cashiers as I chatted away, I swerved momentarily into the other lane.

"*No quiero morir sin amor de una mujer!*" screamed young Roberto from the back seat. Kitty and the men fell into gales of laughter. I asked Kitty to translate.

"Roberto said, 'I don't want to die before I've known the love of a woman!'"

At the Exxon Station we shook hands, thanked the men, and paid them well. We left them standing there. They went back to their world that we'd only peeked into and we went back to ours. Our meeting had been as poignantly meaningful as the ending of T. C. Boyle's marvelous *Tortilla Curtain*. When I told Eric the story he said, "We can only understand other cultures in a one on one relationship."

The next morning the Gooses and I sprang from the back door. They smelled every new bush and tree. Then Gus stalked the giant cypress. Slowly, ever so slowly, he walked around it in a pointer stance! When he returned to the beginning, he raised his little leg and sprinkled it. The new landscape was anointed.

\#

The hours between three and six in the afternoon were the time when the Gooses were most likely to go potty in the house. So I decided to put them in the outdoor pen. Although my vet had recommended a protective top to deter the wildlife, there were limits to what I could afford to do. So every now and then, I'd wrap my head around the back door and count: one, two. I was relieved to see that neither dog had dug out and nothing more threatening than a leaf had fallen inside.

Around six o'clock I went outside to retrieve them. I looked in the pen and saw two creatures I didn't recognize. All three of us were shocked.

"What did you do . . . to yourselves?" I blurted out.

They looked like black-faced minstrels, covered in mud with only the whites of their eyes showing. All they needed was a song and dance routine to complete their transformation. Their little legs were dark brown. They moved up and down in the mud like pistons in an engine, making sucking sounds. The Gooses had dug many holes that had filled with water. After all the landscaping, they were covered in mud!

Yet, I could almost hear them saying . . .

"Mom, just look at Gus! He's made a mess of himself."

"Look at Luc! What's happened to her?"

This was their first encounter with mud-play and like little children they thought it was just so much fun. But at the same time, they were surprised to be wet and dirty. Their innocence and wonder coupled with their complete transformation gave me the best laugh I'd had in a long time.

Chapter Fourteen
Things Fall Apart

In June the Gooses were fourteen months old, and I was seven hundred and twenty-eight months old. The summer people were arriving in greater numbers as the blooms of the rhododendron faded and the mountain laurel brought forth deep, pink blossoms. The scent of native honeysuckle wafted through the house. The peonies in my garden burst open, adding lush beauty to the yard as well as cut flowers for the house.

I'd read that decorating a small room with oversized furniture makes it look larger. So at the end of the kitchen where a table would normally be, I'd replaced the gnawed-on green sofa with two new over-stuffed red sofas. They gave the area a warm and cozy feeling.

Arriving home from church one Sunday, I was amazed to see a six-inch-thick, three-foot wide cushion from the new sofa resting on the floor.

"How did you do this? I just don't understand. And why!"

Then I saw a cavernous hole the dogs had chewed in the frame. "No! I can't believe you have done this! You are destroying my house! I can't afford you!"

When I called the breeder to discuss the incident, she said, "They musta been bored."

"Bored! They had each other to play with, a zoo of stuffed animals, and some KONGs to chew on! They prefer zippers, sofa cushions, and foam! You can now see the floor through the bottom of sofa! My brand new red sofa!"

"Have you tried one of those puzzle toys for dogs left . . ."

I didn't want to hear it! Whatever I did to squelch the dogs' bad behaviors, there seemed to be one more thing to buy, one more suggestion to try, one more command to teach. If I had left them in their pens for five hours, they would have pooped, tinkled, and then sat in it. Sunday school, an hour and half of church, and lunch out totaled five hours away from home.

Although Heidi's training techniques worked well with Gus, Lucy's refusal to obey remained a mystery. I'd decided that in addition to disliking me, she wasn't very smart. When I called her to come inside, I stood with my mouth agape as she ran across the backyard or slowly inched behind a tree, pretending to be deaf—another challenging schnauzer trait. My greatest insight into her behavior came when I read that dogs can be willful. And I'd like to add stubborn. She understood the commands but didn't want to obey—so she didn't!

#

With the long-awaited spring weather at hand, I'd opened the doors to the front deck. The Gooses patrolled the neighborhood with even greater ferocity than last summer. Gus rarely napped during the day and Lucy had acquired his high-strung temperament. They both existed on code orange. The settle-command that had worked so well for Heidi training her German shepherds caused the schnauzers to dance around.

In the evenings Gus continued to attack dogs and horses on the TV screen and Lucy joined in. Every fifteen minutes one of them went to the back door, indicating he needed to be leashed for a potty trip. If I let them outside alone, they'd run to Sam's house and bark at him through his sliding glass door: "How dare you sit in your own house and watch TV! That really pisses us off." I imagined this strange behavior would stop soon, but I saw it as another peculiar challenge of schnauzer ownership. The peace and quiet that I'd so desperately sought by moving to the mountains was gone from my life.

#

I volunteer at church to become a part of a community of faith. At the end of a parish life meeting, the chairman Anne Norman asked if anyone was interested in writing The Episcopal Church of the Incarnation's first cookbook. Many sane people who had previous experience on a cookbook committee resigned. So it was the novices who began the task. After the first organizational meeting where we simply sought to name the book—a two-hour exercise without closure—I could see where we were headed but my sense of duty kept me returning. I learned many good cooks are very creative but not well-organized. I kept telling myself, "Just one more meeting and I'll have them moving ahead in the right direction." That would be the contribution of a lack-luster cook.

Over the next several weeks, the cookbook committee became a snowball that mowed me down. I realized that putting myself first so I could live the life God gave me was going to be something I mastered on a daily basis. As the cookbook committee absorbed more and more of my time and mental ability, my dog dilemma reached a crisis.

#

"I'm at the end of my rope!" I said to Dr. Ransom when the Gooses arrived for their fourteen-month check-up.

"Let me ask the questions. Then I'll answer yours," he said. Gus had had his usual bowel movement in the reception area, joining the notorious pack of dogs that always poop at the vet's office. But, had taken the stance of a Westminster champion on the examining table. Dr. Ransom rattled off what seemed like thousands of questions as I gave one-syllable replies.

At this point in my schnauzer ownership, I wasn't in the mood for more rules. I couldn't keep up with all the ones I had been told to follow. I didn't want to be a Sergeant-at-Arms in my golden years. I didn't find it amusing when people told me stories about how dogs outsmarted their owners. I wanted relief. I wanted out. I wanted a clean house more than I wanted two dogs!

"You and these dogs are a terrible match!" announced Dr. Ransom, asserting a belief diametrically opposed to his original opinion.

"I totally agree," I responded. "I'm burned out. I'm dogged-out. Yes! That's it—I'm dogged out!"

"You are a nurturer. These dogs need a disciplinarian . . . blah, blah, blah."

I'd heard it all before. Regardless of what Dr. Ransom thought about my having nurtured Gus, I was glad I had done it and thought it had paid off. Gus loved people. Now he could accept a firmer hand of discipline from someone else. My Einstein-dog would catch on quickly.

"You can't just walk them. They need to be on a treadmill thirty minutes every day."

For the past six months, I'd tried to get myself back on the treadmill for thirty minutes every day. As far as the Gooses went, I pictured neurotic Gus on the treadmill trying to keep pace so the machine wouldn't eat him alive. Knowing her turn was coming up next, Lucy would be hiding under the Sheridan sofa in the living room.

"And what about me, Dr. Ransom?" I shouted. "I helped my husbands and children build their lives and finally at the age of fifty, I began to live mine. I stopped teaching and began to study oil painting. What about how I want to spend the remainder of my days? I want to live in the Dordogne! Eat fruits and vegetables in season! Get a suntan with the accompanying lines and wrinkles! And die without medical intervention!"

He stared at me, speechless.

"As far as dogs go, I just want a dog like the ones I had in the past. A dog that always comes when he's called because he loves having my attention; a dog that is content to sit on a sofa without eating it. A dog that hops in the car because he's pleased to be offered a ride. A dog that rides around without throwing up in my pocketbook! A dog that is so easily house-trained I have little memory of it!"

"I'm concerned about you," Dr. Ransom injected. "You need to remember that dogs live in the moment and adjust easily to new situations. You can find homes for them if that's what you want. In a few months they won't even remember you!"

"Look, I don't want to agree with your assessment of how Gus and Lucy will forget me. Yet, I know the three of us needed something that I couldn't provide," I paused. "Do you think getting litter mates attributed to my predicament?"

"Probably," he answered.

"There's no doubt the Gooses bonded to each other and pay very little attention to me. Like Bonnie and Clyde, these dogs have been driving around my house in an old jalopy creating mayhem. I've had enough!" and I screamed, a short little out-of-control scream that felt really good!

When Eric called that evening, I explained that I was on overload. Resolving the dog situation was primary. He wanted to come for a visit, but I needed to keep my mind clear.

"I'm sorry, dear friend. The dogs come first."

#

My retired friends adored their dogs; in fact, they'd quickly become replacement-children, filling their deep void to nurture a loved one. Clearly, Gus and Lucy were my last children. I had to acknowledge I felt so close to the Gooses; I knew them so well—better than any of my "family dogs." I was amazed at how deeply I loved them; they felt a part of me. With them, I was no longer alone in these desolate mountains.

When I discussed giving away the Gooses with the trainer, she said they shouldn't be separated; but the vet and my daughter disagreed. The axiom, "They play off each other acquiring the other's bad habits," seemed to describe the behavior I'd witnessed. So I concluded they would be better-behaved and happier dogs if they lived in separate homes.

As I saw it, I had three options. Option number one was for Sadie to take the Gooses back and find homes for them. My second option was the Cashiers-Highlands Humane Society. It was an outstanding no-kill center, and most of the people who adopted dogs were well-educated and well-to-do. I knew that they would take good care of Gus and Lucy. The third option was to find two friends who would take one of the Gooses, knowing that separating them would solve most of their behavior problems.

Although the three options were rational, the thought of giving my babies away caused me to cry uncontrollably for days on end. This break-up was raining every emotion that I'd experienced during times of great loss. Once again, I was immobilized by my feelings. For weeks I'd put off making the phone calls that would begin the break up of my family. When I thought about taking them on our last ride together—

hopefully, to a friend's house—the memory of driving Mother from Piedmont Hospital to Atlanta Hospice jumped up in my mind and I sobbed.

Fortunately, I've come to realize that when I'm in a relationship that is harmful to me, I feel conflicted. Like all of God's creatures, I want to love as well as be loved. But life has brought wisdom and the strength to let go and feel the pain of loss. I had to put my needs before those of my pets, believing this strategy would result in a better life for all three of us. I told myself to stay focused on that fact. At long last, I was number one.

Chapter Fifteen
The Love of My Life

Anne, the cookbook chairwoman, had been offering to take Gus for a few days. Her exact words were *to give you some relief.* Digging out of my emotional quandary, I was finally able to ask the pertinent question, "Are you thinking about keeping him?"

"Yes. You know, my husband and I've been looking for a dog. What you've said about Gus makes me think he'd be a good match for us. He sounds like quite a character . . . one with a lot of energy."

"Yes, that's Gus," I said. "It's Friday afternoon. What if I bring him to you Monday at 5:00?"

Anne agreed. I thought this could be an ideal solution. I knew the Normans would be good parents for Gus. I rejoiced that he would live nearby, and I could visit him often. Lucy would be easier to place; a single woman would be a great mom for her—just not this dogged-out single woman.

Later, I wondered what I'd said about Gus that made Anne think he would be a good match for her family, a married couple with three grown daughters? I would have thought what I'd said would have struck fear into the hearts of dog owners everywhere. He has nervous bowel movements. Is house-trained until 5:00 P.M. Loves a twenty-minute romp around the neighborhood preferably while it's sleeting. Also, I had mentioned that Gus possessed a proclivity for home demolition. Of course, he had his good traits. He was highly intelligent, full of personality, and a stunningly beautiful dog.

When Anne agreed to try Gus out, I knew the next three days were going to be our last time together. The last Saturday, Sunday, and Monday for Gus, Lucy, and me. My unbreakable family was going to be broken. I planned slow, calm times. Days of drinking in the love that had bonded us during the past fourteen months.

On Monday I typed up directions for how to care for Gus. When I finished, it was two typed pages. It began, "Call me anytime and I will come get him." On the first page, I suggested we'd take three weeks to decide. At any juncture, the Normans could give Gus back and I could ask that he be returned.

While I bathed Gus, I began to wonder if Lucy, a more even-tempered dog, would be a better match for them. They would probably have grandchildren one day. I had reservations as to how high-strung Gus might interact with a young child. So I bathed Lucy, too. I had the nastiest feeling in my stomach that said I was getting my children ready for their foster parents' approval. But I continued with the preparations for Gus to be re-homed, a term that indicated there wasn't anything innately wrong with the dogs or me, but together we didn't function well.

That afternoon the sun streamed in from the French doors as Gus, Lucy, and I lounged on my bed. Gus put his head on my feet and I patted him. His head fit perfectly in the palm of my hand. *How can I give him away?* Because I had asked Sadie for a silver schnauzer, Gus had been mine since his conception. The princess was aloof, sitting on one of the many pillows. At times, I cried and the dogs came to me. I marveled at how they knew that there was something terribly wrong. Reason prevailed, but emotionally I needed Gus, needed our family of three. I needed to continue to take care of someone, and realized that someone was me.

Re-homing Gus would be so difficult for him. He would have so many adjustments to make. I thought about all the time and energy I had put into making this little dog feel secure and knew that over the next few months his life would be in turmoil.

Around 4:30 I began loading the car with Gus's possessions: his crate containing his comforter; his toys, including the two George W. dolls; an envelope with his heartworm pill, and his instruction sheet. Then I went inside for Gus. Both Gooses were at the back door, looking up at me inquisitively. I looked down and saw they were nose to nose for the last time. I ached as I reached into this happy scene and pulled Gus out. I attached his leather leash to his studded black collar, the one that made the little fellow feel like a testosterone-filled boxer.

As I walked him to the car, thunder cracked. The sky darkened and rain began to pour down. For the first time, Gus was frightened by a thunderstorm. From his perspective, sitting in the front seat surrounded by the windows, he was in the storm. As I drove out of the neighborhood, Gus cowered; he pressed his body into the back of the seat, his head hung low, his eyes downcast. I'd never seen Gus like this. I began to cry. For me, it was now or never. I couldn't repeat today. So I rubbed Gus's little head and spoke to him softly.

"Don't be scared, my boy. It's just a rainstorm."

But Gus began to shake. The lightning crackled and the thunder boomed. Shards of silver streaked down from the sky.

"We're going to try something . . . a new adventure with different people and interesting new odors. The Normans have been looking for a dog. Carl jogs and Anne is always on the go. I think they will be better parents for you. Your life will be more fun than if you stayed with me and were house-bound most days."

I looked down at Gus and realized the cruelest part of giving him away: I couldn't explain it to him. The mom who had always been there for him was leaving him. I couldn't offer any words of comfort. He would have to live through the transition of meeting new caretakers, feeling alone, and adjusting to a new home.

"This is a King Solomon's gift that I give you—a better life."

I stopped at the grocery store to buy dog food for Gus and lemon ice cream for me; these were today's necessities. The beauty of our area that usually lifted my spirits wasn't having any effect. As I drove up Holt Knob, I saw the Normans' yard edged with a white picket fence and the garden filled with hollyhocks and roses. The rain had stopped. Gus happily hopped out of the car. We made our way to the front door and rang the bell. Anne opened the door and exclaimed, "He's adorable! Come on in."

Anne and Carl were having drinks.

"Would you like a glass of wine?" Carl asked.

"Yes!" I answered. Carl poured a glass of Chardonnay while Gus left a fresh pile of smelly poop near the door to the deck. I jumped up and went for the paper towels.

"I'm so sorry," I said. It *was* 5:00 P.M.

But the Normans waved it off. We chatted as Gus investigated the living room. Then he ran over to me and stood on his hind legs to lick the condensation off my wine glass.

As I read Gus's instruction sheet aloud, Carl reached down and picked him up, lifting him over his head. Gus smiled down and looked Carl in the eye; they were two guys enjoying each other. Gus had found his man, and Carl had a male companion in his family of all women.

I went out to the car and brought in Gus's pen and toys. Returning to the house, I leaned over, took his little head in my hands and kissed him. I had an aching lump in my throat. I waved goodbye to the Normans and walked out the door without looking back. I couldn't have borne the look on Gus's face as I left him. I knew it would appear and reappear in my PTSD mind. In my plaintive state, I started to cry. I pulled into a vacant parking lot and sobbed for my boy.

When I arrived home, Lucy looked stunned as she questioned me with her chestnut eyes, "Where's Gus? He always comes home with you." I turned away. Lucy trotted off to look for him in the garage. Then she went to the outdoor pen. Confused, she came back inside. Leaving her alone in the kitchen that night was unthinkable. We slept together.

I awoke to a little black nose nudging mine.

"Lucy, I think you like it here."

After I fed her, I let her out to potty. Again, she looked for Gus in the outdoor pen and then in the garage.

"Lucy, Gus has gone to live with the Normans," I said, tears streaming down my cheeks.

The house was quiet for the first time in months. I missed Gus *so* much. I wished I'd kept him. But the peace that I had longed for had been restored. It seemed as if six dogs had moved out. There weren't any "dogfights," times when the Gooses would jump on each other, growl, and bark. As the day progressed, Lucy didn't dart out an opened door because my attention was focused on Gus. She wasn't going postal when she heard an unfamiliar noise.

Through my pain of missing Gus, every now and then, I had a panic-stricken thought: What if the Normans called and asked me to take him back? I was loving the peace and quiet; my highly reactive mind loved it, too. My rattled memory had less to remember. Because I knew Gus so well, I knew he'd charm his way into Normans's hearts. My little guy was gone forever. Later that day, Anne phoned to say that Gus was fine. By the way, she thought I'd like to know he was house-trained. Kind woman that she was, she called every day over the next three weeks. She told me how well Gus was doing, what a good mother I had been to have raised such a fine dog, and how much they loved him. I couldn't have wished for more.

When the three-week trial period ended, the Normans decided to keep Gus. They said, "He's a great dog! He brings joy and laughter into our life."

#

The emotional turmoil of giving Gus away proved to be far greater than the experience of having my previous dog, Meredith, put to sleep. Her life had ended in the vet's office with me holding her as she was anesthetized into death. When her head dropped unnaturally, I sobbed. I had mourned her death as a normal part of dog ownership. But re-homing was more like a divorce involving children. A divorce that didn't end a relationship but changed it. There wasn't an end to my strong, loving, and protective feelings for Gus. To be perfectly honest, the Normans put up with me being an obnoxious, overbearing former parent for years to come.

My most surprising insight about love and loving Gus was his love for me was pure. He didn't love me as if I were a charm on a bracelet or as someone he could get something from, but simply for who I was. Ours was a relationship in the simplest sense of the word. That's the reason he's the love of my life.

As the days passed, I missed Gus less and less. But as the weeks passed and I forgot his bad behavior, I missed him more and more until I didn't have any tears left except for an occasional gulp of sorrow at night when I lay in bed longing to hold my boy in my arms.

Chapter Sixteen
The Hedonist

In July a couple of weeks after Gus's departure, I arrived at church and was greeted by Nell's husband, Bill. "Good morning. How're you doing?"

"I'm fine, thank you."

"I didn't know you were giving the dogs away," Bill said, grimacing.

"Yes. I'm dogged-out. The cleanup and destruction have been appalling. If you know of anyone who'd like Lucy, please let me know. The Normans have Gus."

"Oh, I knew that. They brought him to a dinner party last night. We were sitting in the Sloanes' ornate living room."

"Yeah." I froze.

"You know, it's decorated in fine fabrics, fragile antiques, and a collection of Chinese export porcelain. Their Frabel collection and Chihuly shells are just scattered around."

I stopped breathing.

"We were chatting and sipping cocktails. When, all of a sudden, Gus jumped up on the coffee table and peed in a tureen!" Bill said, laughing.

"That's my boy!"

#

Except for my longing to touch Gus and to play with him, to have given him to the Normans worked well for everyone. He has become a calmer and happier dog, which has equated to being a well-behaved dog. Under Anne's tutelage, he's been trained. More importantly, he's gained his autonomy and feels comfortable where ever he is—even boarding at the vet's. He loves to jog five miles with Carl on Saturday mornings, alleviating some of his excess energy. When left at home alone, Gus has been known to chew up a shoe and then enter his pen and close the door. Also, he's acquired the ability to run the windows down in both of the Normans' cars; this could be a life-saving skill for a dog belonging to an older couple. He's learned to tell time. Close to 6 P.M., Gus will begin to dance and bark, indicating it's time for his second feeding. If his behavior goes unnoticed, he picks up his food bowl and drops it at Anne's feet. Gus enjoys being in the town of Highlands where the houses are close together; everyone loves a visit from him. And he is fond of his neighbor Megan, a Corgi puppy.

When I visit the Normans, I say, "Hi, Gus Goose. How's my boy?"

He recognizes my voice and squeals. He knows the Normans don't ask him to behave when I'm there. We're both naughty. Gus jumps up on me and I rub his body. Then his little tongue begins to slither in and out searching for my mouth.

"No, Gus, I know where that tongue has been!" I sit down and he runs around the living room several times and then stops in front of me before rolling onto his back, little black eyes darting from side to side. "Tummy rub, Mom?" I sit on the floor next to him and rub. He falls asleep on his back. He is a happy dog.

#

Because giving Gus to friends worked so well, I suggested to others that they might enjoy having Lucy. But they simply replied, "You're preaching to the choir."

A year earlier in the respite of September, I had been deciding whether or not to neuter my puppies, and the thought of giving them away hadn't entered my mind. If I tried to understand how I'd come to this, I would blame myself for not being a better trainer, blame the schnauzers for being a challenging breed to train, but blaming was a waste of good energy. So onward I went, keeping in mind the good things that had come from re-homing Gus.

I registered Lucy with the Cashiers-Highlands Humane Society as I continued to search for a home for her. Because the shelter was full, I was permitted to keep her at home and screen the interested parties over the phone. So far, I hadn't found the right match. However, I was enjoying having only one dog. And after her initial adjustment, the princess was enjoying having all my attention—so typical of royalty.

#

"Where's Mr. Gus?" Mr. Peters shouted from his backyard. "I haven't seen him for a while. You know, him's my favorite. The missus and I are still laughing at how funny he looked in him's George W. costume last Halloween."

"I gave Gus to the Normans, friends at church. Their active life-style suits him better. I adore Gus. I miss him more than I'd have thought possible."

"I get it. A couple of years ago, lost my best huntin' dog to a bear. Went into a deep depression. Drank for days."

"That's so sad."

"Mrs. P. about threw me out."

"I doubt that! After years of raising hound dogs, do you have any advice on house-training Lucy?"

"Well, I think that Lucy's confused about being a dog. Jest trust her to take care of herself when she goes outside. Walk that little dog twice a day. She'll shit and do number one."

"You're probably right."

"You forgits her's a dog! Under all them clothes and that sweet-smelling powder, Lucy is jest a dog."

And up from the cobwebs of my mind came a powerful insight: I want Lucy to be a child, because I want to be a mother who's still raising her daughter. To see her every day. To spoil her. To be there for her. To know now what I didn't know then—how hard life can be. Digesting my myriad of thoughts and regrets, I remembered Mr. Peters' statement: Lucy is jest a dog.

#

Taking Mr. Peters' advice, I began to walk Lucy twice a day and she was happy to eliminate. But there were other times when I'd left her at home for many hours, and another Lake Pontchartrain greeted me. That seemed to indicate she knew not to go potty in the house but couldn't hold her urine any longer. Our vet had proclaimed Lucy to be a healthy schnauzer. But I wondered if there was a physical reason for her problem. I needed a second opinion.

Everyone I knew spoke very highly of the young vets at the Rabun Animal Hospital in Mountain City, Georgia. So I called and made an appointment. When I arrived at the large red brick building, I noticed that one side of the facility was designated for dogs and the other for cats. Inside a slew of receptionists and technicians manned a twenty-foot counter. They were signing people in, checking them out, giving out meds, and delivering results of lab tests.

My appointment was with Dr. Brad Smith. After a short wait Lucy and I were ushered into an examining room. In a few minutes Dr. Brad, a large, attractive man with a sweet smile, arrived with his assistant.

I explained, "Lucy has been very difficult to house-train. In fact, she still has accidents. I'm wondering if there's a medical reason."

"Let's put her up on the table and take a look," Dr. Brad said.

We looked down at Lucy. She was performing a tipped-cow imitation, lying on her side pressing into the floor.

"I want a normal dog," I mumbled as I leaned over and tried to pry her loose, wedging my fingers under her body.

But I wasn't strong enough to lift her. Surprising Lucy, Dr. Brad pulled her up and plopped her on the table. Her shocked expression seemed to say, "Oh, perhaps this doctor knows how to deal with my pranks."

Dr. Brad chatted with me as he examined Lucy. "I may have found the problem. I'm going to do a urinalysis. Be back in a minute."

"Take your time." After all Lucy and I 'd been through, there seemed to be an answer. And one that didn't involve more training or purchasing a new gadget. Just a marvelous young vet!

Returning to the examining room, Dr. Brad announced, "Lucy has an inverted vulva . . .

"A what?" I interrupted.

"An inverted vulva that has contributed to a severe urinary-tract infection. There's blood in her urine."

"That sounds serious. Blood in her urine."

Dr. Brad nodded.

"What is an inverted vulva?" I asked, feeling her pain.

"Her vulva is turned inside out. It catches germs from her feces. The germs have traveled to her urinary track. When the infection is gone, I'll operate and re-build the vulva, making it the way nature intended. After she's been on the antibiotics for two weeks, I want you to catch some urine for me."

"Catch some urine?" I repeated, confused.

"Yes, it's very easy. Here's a little cup. You take her outside to potty and when she stoops, just slide this cup under her rear legs and catch the urine."

"Sounds simple enough."

Dr. Brad put Lucy on antibiotics, changed her food so that her system wouldn't be too acidic, and added a dietary supplement. I took out a second mortgage.

Lucy loved her new food, especially the canned Prescription Diet. After she was on the regimen for two weeks, I took her outside. As she stooped, I tried to slide the two-inch cup under her rear. But once I had touched her, up she went. So typical of Lucy, she refused to squat again. Now she was going to hold her urine! I called Dr. Brad's office and reported my failure. He told me to bring Lucy down and let the professionals have a try. But once again, when Lucy's rear was touched, she bounced up and didn't squat again.

Later, I noticed that the take-home cup had a small red cap that I might be able to slide between her back legs without her noticing. During my next dash down the mountain to let the professionals have another try, I remembered Lucy would urinate whenever a stranger leaned over to pat her. She'd lower her head, squat, and tinkle—still the submissive urinator.

When I arrived at the clinic, I parked the car and grabbed Lucy's leash. I ran into the office and threw open the gate that separates the patients from the staff. Everyone stared at us; they probably thought Lucy needed emergency treatment.

"Would someone come here and pat her?" I shouted. Now everyone looked puzzled. Meagan, one of the assistants, came over. Lucy looked up, saw the hand coming down on her head and squatted, delivering a pool of urine. Some fell into the red cap! Our audience looked at Lucy's urine with displeasure, but Megan and I were delighted to have found a technique that worked.

Unfortunately, Lucy still had the persistent infection. Over the next several months, this same scene played out over and over again. One time when I called to tell the clinic we were on our way, the technician who answered the phone said, "Oh! She's *that* one."

Three months later, Lucy was cured of the urinary tract infection and ready for surgery. Dr. Brad had performed a number of inverted vulva procedures with very good results. However, he warned me that this surgery would be more complicated and more painful than when she was spayed.

Lucy's surgery went well, and I was relieved that she spent that painful first night at the vet's office. The following day she came home wearing a cone on her head that prevented her from removing the stitches. The stitches formed an inverted U-shape on her rear; each had been individually tied. Dr. Brad had done a beautiful job.

Whether Lucy was awake or asleep, we spent the next ten days together. If I allowed her to sit on the floor and scoot around, she would pull out the stitches and shred the tissue. A repair job would be a more difficult procedure than the original surgery. I felt for Lucy. She looked pitiful with that plastic cone on her head, but she didn't appear to mind. I thought perhaps the pain from her undiagnosed urinary tract infection accounted for her sour attitude. Whereas, being stubborn and willful were part of her personality. In a couple of weeks, she'd recovered fully from the surgery.

Knowing that no one wants an unhouse-trained dog, I moved the dog pen back into the house, devoid of the comforter, toys, and food. Lucy pranced in. Crate training had begun! Training was now a term I understood. Lucy would be in the crate when I left the house. No more half-eaten sofas, no more pools of urine, no more treasured books shredded for kindling.

Whenever Lucy said a very emphatic, *Ah, roo-roo-roo*, the translation was, "I need to potty. Now!" She jumped on the red sofa and threw her front legs over the rolled arm. I attached the leash. Then she reared up on her hind legs and leaped over the arm to the floor, illustrating the energy of a healthy dog. Together, we ventured out to potty as I sang the *Halleluiah Chorus*.

After a great deal of effort on my part and a great deal of pain on Lucy's, she became a house-trained schnauzer. As her health improved, the anger in her bark seemed to dissipate. Instead of her inflamed greeting in the morning, she began to jump up and down, happy to see me. And with her partner in crime gone, she *had* to relate to me.

My bond with her was further deepened when I realized how much she loved being massaged. For a woman with hands in perpetual motion, this was a plus. As I rubbed her tummy, her entire body began to relax. Soon her eyes closed. Then her neck muscles went limp—this signaled her readiness for a chin tickle. Limbs spread eagle, neck back, head swung to one side translated to Lucy being in paradise. As it turned out, she was a hedonist of magnificent proportions! Quite often, as I rubbed her, she noticed that my other hand was idle. Her paw would tap it as if to say, "You know I prefer a two-handed massage!"

Chapter Seventeen
My Last Child

In August I was still dogged-out and searching for a good home for Lucy, unaware of the bond that was being formed between us. While she was recuperating from surgery, she'd added two words to her vocabulary. One was *muurf*. She said it quietly and softly, as if she didn't want to disturb but had a problem she couldn't fix herself. More often than not, there was something in her way or a door wasn't opened wide enough to pass through. Her body image was that of a Shetland Sheepdog.

Her other new word was *rou*; it rhymed with *how* and had a guttural sound. It indicated the princess' great displeasure and the irony of it always made me laugh. It was a haughty, queen-like snarl. She'd lift her upper lip and say, *"Rou!"* The translation was: "I am not pleased!" For a dog upon whom all of life's necessities and pleasures were profusely lavished, *rou* seemed the height of arrogance.

Like the gold-diggers of the Old West, her highness laid claim to the new red sofa, which now she seemed uninterested in eating. I was allowed the matching loveseat. That was our usual configuration for watching TV at night. It was a cold

October evening, and I was dressed up waiting until it was time to leave for a party. I glanced over at Lucy. Her sofa and doggie pad were covered in half a gallon of fuchsia-colored liquid; it was thick, syrupy, and filled with berries. I retrieved her from the mess and put her in the pen. She watched as I performed the cleanup. I mixed Oxy-clean powder with a small amount of water then scrubbed the cushions. I took the doggie pad outside and shook it over the front deck to get rid of the berries; then I dropped it into the washing machine. Afterwards, I mopped the floor and let Lucy out of the pen. The princess was content to assume her position on her sofa.

A few minutes later, I glanced at her. She'd thrown up again. This time, with the doggie pad in the washing machine, she had hit the remaining sofa cushions. I repeated the cleanup. Even though Lucy looked fine, the immense volume of syrupy liquid alarmed me. I didn't think her stomach could have held that much. I couldn't leave her without first speaking to a vet.

I phoned Rabun Animal Hospital and was told that Dr. Patsy was taking emergency calls. She answered the phone as she was leaving the clinic.

"Dr. Patsy, I have a schnauzer named Lucy. She's eaten some berries. They look really potent. They're a deep fuchsia color. Do you have any idea what they might be?"

"No, I don't. How's Lucy acting?"

"She's thrown up twice, but seems fine now. There can't be much left in her stomach," I said. "Maybe we could ask a vet who hikes if he's seen these berries."

"I can't think of a vet who hikes. Does Lucy have any other symptoms?"

"No, she doesn't," I said. "Maybe we could go on-line?" I realized that Dr. Patsy was the methodically minded scientist while I was the increasingly alarmed dog owner. As we were chatting, Dr. Patsy was walking back into the clinic.

"I'm on-line now. Do you still have the berries?"

"No, but I can describe them to you."

"Go ahead."

"They're the size of blueberries, almost black in color. Dimpled, not smooth, but that may be because they were partially digested. The liquid is thick. It soaked into the sofa cushions like dye."

"I think I know what Lucy ate. There's a photo of a vine with big, irregular green leaves. The veins are fuchsia."

"I think you're right! I've seen those bushes in my yard. There's one near the garage."

"They're pokeberries. There's a blog written by a vet. He says they are very poisonous to dogs. How fast can you get her here?"

"Forty-five minutes. I'll get there as quick as I can!"

When I put Lucy's leash on, she didn't jump around as she usually did. She stood still, very still. I drove like a wild woman down the mountain to Dillard, Georgia, and made a left turn onto Rt. 441. Lucy had been poisoned, and I couldn't do anything to help except get her to the clinic as quickly as possible.

There weren't any streetlights on the little country road. I was extremely nearsighted with the added challenge of undiagnosed cataracts. I knew that I wouldn't be able to read the street sign for the clinic, but I was hoping that I could see their large sign on the corner of the road. I knew to turn in front of it. Driving at night confused me. I had to stop and ask if I'd passed the Animal Hospital. As I got back in the car, Lucy was still. Had she slipped into a coma? Had she died? I patted her head. She moved slightly.

With my blood pressure rising, I drove past the city limit sign for Mountain City. I called into the back seat to see if I could arouse her, "Lucy, we're almost there. It won't be much longer! Lucy!" I screamed the last *Lucy*. Her head bobbed up but quickly fell to the seat.

"The sign! There it is in a farmer's field. I found it, Luc!"

"Turn in front, turn in front," I whispered to myself. I slowed the car down to a crawl in order not to disturb Lucy and made the turn as smoothly as a BMW. As I drove into the large parking lot, I was surprised to see Dr. Patsy and her assistant standing there.

"I've had a chance to read more about pokeberries. They are extremely poisonous to dogs," announced Dr. Patsy.

I took Lucy from the car and carefully placed her on the pavement. She stood up and wobbled into the clinic. When Dr. Patsy reached down and patted her, she tinkled a two-foot wide circle of fuchsia urine.

"That's a first for me," said Dr. Patsy.

"Uuuuug," said the assistant, pointing to the urine.

"That's it! That's the color of the pokeberry juice!" I said, feeling better just to be there.

"We'll need to do a tox-screen. Then I'll give her charcoal water to leech out the toxins. Do you think she'll drink it?" asked Dr. Patsy.

"I don't see why not. When she's outside, she eats acorns, bark chips, and baby birds. Inside she eats quarter round and sheet rock. Compared to those, charcoal water will taste like a smoothie."

I was dismissed. Lucy entered the bowels of the veterinary clinic. I drove further south to Ingles to buy more Oxy-clean and then home. I went to bed but couldn't sleep, because I was so worried about Lucy. She had become my best friend. Lucy being poisoned to the point of near death had shown me how much I loved her and treasured sharing my days with this sweet, adoring dog. Her humor and joy lightened my footsteps. I couldn't possibly part with her.

In the morning I called the clinic and was told that Lucy had come through her ordeal. She would live! I could pick her up.

When I arrived, Dr. Patsy appeared with Lucy on a leash. "She drank all the charcoal water. She's such a good dog. I think she may be my favorite schnauzer!"

"That's great. She is very sweet and quite a character! Thank you so much." I paid the bill; it was over three hundred dollars. And took the pokeberry pooch home to recuperate. She slept for most of the day on her favorite down-filled sofa in my office.

That evening Lucy hopped on her red sofa, managing not to fall through the hole she and Gus had chewed in its frame. She noticed that the cushions were missing. Not pleased, her highness turned to me and said, *"Rou!"*

"You know, Luc, the pokeberry stain came out of the sofa cushions, but they're still wet. Big picture—you're lucky to be alive!"

But her highness looked up at me, raised her upper lip, and said, *"Rou!"*

And I laughed. Happy to be Lucy's mom.

It's that lovely, slow month. I'm feeling tired. It seems decadent to watch a movie during daylight hours. But perhaps that is just what these latter years are for. I put a DVD of *Miss Potter* into my computer. It's the biography of Beatrix Potter, woman writer living in the mountains of England's Lake District. I go downstairs and get my bed pillows. Prop them on the office sofa, lie down, and whistle for Lucy. She bounds up the stairs and jumps on the sofa with me. Puts her head on my pillow and stretches out on her side as she presses her back into me. I tickle her chest and she rolls slightly, offering up her tummy. I rub for a few minutes and then stop. She raises her head and stares in my eyes which means, "Not finished, are you?"

I look into her chestnut eyes and ask, "Are you sure you're a dog?"

As the movie plays, I fall asleep and dream. Gus, Lucy, and I are living in the Dordogne, lush and green like my hometown of Atlanta. I eat fruits and vegetables in season. I get a suntan with the accompanying lines and wrinkles. I pick orchids by the roadside. Best of all, the Gooses eliminate where they stand on a dusty old road in verdant France.

EPILOGUE

Although it has been six years since Gus lived with us, Lucy still recognizes his name. If we're at home when I mention him, she squeals and looks out the window. If we're visiting him on Holt Knob, she greets him with a few sniffs and immediately calms down. That's how she displays love. When Gus barks at her, he seems to be saying, "You have Mother Goose all the time. When she comes here, she's mine!"

One of the Normans neighbors, the Adams, host an annual party for friends and their dogs. Not being acquainted with them, the Normans weren't invited. In fact, it was Gus who entered the house when the front door opened. Having learned the ropes of human behavior, he walked up to a group of guests, sat down, and held out his paw.

"Cute dog! Wants to shake hands," murmured a guest.

After the handshake, Gus was rewarded with an appetizer. He continued to work his way through the crowd, exhibiting his show dog spirit.

As well as attending cocktail parties, Gus has traveled to many states in the Southeast. Savannah, the Normans' second home, is Gus's favorite destination. He likes to sit in a bay window of their townhouse and bark at the horse-drawn carriages. As he rides around town, he continues his futile pursuit of the horses, much to the amusement of the tourists. One asked Anne, "What's your dog goin' to do with a horse if he gets him?"

It was a cold December day when Gus saw the ocean for the first time on Tybee Island near Savannah. Arriving at the beach, the Normans took his leash off and let him run. He noticed a tidal pool and waded in. With each step, the water crawled up his body until only his head and neck were visible. Gus froze, looking like the closet thing to the Loch Ness monster Tybee Island had ever seen. Anne and Carl called to him as a small crowd gathered and aimed their camera-phones at Gus.

"Carl, you're going to have to get him," Anne shouted. But not liking attention tossed his way, Carl continued to call to Gus. He remained a frozen silver head. Finally relinquishing his stance, Carl took off his shoes and socks and rolled up his khakis. He wadded in, arms outstretched. Reaching under the icy water, Carl retrieved Gus's soaking-wet body and carried him to shore. Much to Carl's chagrin, a member of the local TV news team had filmed the rescue!

In 2013 the Normans moved to Pinehurst, North Carolina, five hours east of Highlands. I considered moving with them. As I'm typing, Gus and Lucy are asleep on my office floor. Although Gus is exhausted and confused about the move— he now lives in their car not wanting to miss the exit. His autonomy and training will serve him well in our mobile world. He will introduce the Normans to a city filled with new friends while Lucy and I remain in Highlands, delightfully co-dependant and adoring of one another.

News Flash: January 2015. The Norman's are returning to Highlands. Gus Goose is coming home to Momma!

ACKNOWLEDGEMENT

With deepest gratitude to Gene Young, Susan Leon, and Linda Hobson for editing the manuscript.

COVER

With deepest gratitude to Pamela Warr for the cover design, and to Graham A. Morrison and Helen Moore for the photographs.

Visit us on Facebook at Isabel MacRae Allen's group, *Outnumbered*. Tell me your dog's adventures

DISCUSSION QUESTIONS FOR BOOK CLUBS

1. What were the problems Isabel was dealing with when trying to train Gus and Lucy?

2. When were Isabel's heart and mind in conflict? Have you ever had to make a similar decision?

3. Which dog was the most challenging adversary? Which did Isabel love more? Which was your favorite?

4. Name some of the plethora of wildlife marching through Isabel's yard. Do you think she was ever at peace with these visitors?

5. Was there a time when you thought the focus of your life was your spouse and children to the neglect of yourself?

Author Note: The cover of *Outnumbered* shows Lucy on the left and Gus on the right.

Made in the USA
Lexington, KY
17 November 2015